SICK OF SUFFERING

SICK OF SUFFERING

A Radical New Guide to
Healing Your Brain
and Getting Your Life Back

EVAN MICHAEL YORK

LIONCREST
PUBLISHING

SICK OF SUFFERING
*A Radical New Guide to Healing Your Brain
and Getting Your Life Back*

ISBN   978-1-61961-745-2 *Paperback*
       978-1-61961-746-9 *Ebook*

To Marjorie Bergman,
a woman who truly cares for people and
is always willing to figure it out.
Thank you for saving my life.

CONTENTS

———

INTRODUCTION

———

Many young adults, particularly college students, struggle with mental health problems, chiefly anxiety and depression, and have no idea where to turn for help. I know this from experience because it was my story. In college, I went through a long period of chronic anxiety and depression, and I felt as if I was searching in the dark for answers. If this is your story, too, then this book is for you.

I encounter many people on a daily basis who struggle with mental and emotional health. Friends go through it. A former roommate of mine went through it. They don't know what's causing these problems, and they have no idea how to fix them. What they've tried hasn't worked, so they assume they're damned to a life of mental health crises.

I should clarify that there are some kinds of anxiety that are perfectly normal—for example, being anxious about school or work. If you have a big test coming up, it's normal to worry about it a little bit. That's not what I'm referring to. I'm referring, instead, to people who deal with chronic anxiety every single day. They wake up with it, and the feeling isn't connected to anything that's happening in their lives—nothing they can pinpoint—but it's there.

Sick and miserable, they feel as if they're losing control of their lives, and they have no idea what's wrong or where to turn. This kind of anxiety is not normal, it's not natural, and it's not something you should have to live with.

Unfortunately, anxiety and depression often go hand in hand, so many people who deal with one also deal with the other. These people feel a constant sense of dread. They've lost interest in things they are supposed to be doing and things they once cared about. School, work, and relationships suffer as a result. That's not normal, either. Life is not supposed to be that way.

In a few cases, these feelings are symptoms of a severe mental health problem that needs to be addressed by a health-care professional and intensive treatment. However, I believe that in most cases—the overwhelming majority of cases—people who are suffering from anxiety, depression, and other mental health problems could resolve them by making a few key lifestyle changes.

THE MIND/BODY CONNECTION

As a college student, I suddenly found myself flooded with anxiety and depression on a daily basis, and I had no idea of the cause. I assumed it was all in my head, and that something was going haywire with my brain. What never occurred to me is that my mental health problems were the result of something wrong with my body. Like most people, I had never made the connection between mental health and physical health.

What people fail to realize is that our physical being comprises both our mental state and our physical state; they are intimately connected. We are, in our entirety, both of those things, and they influence one another. What you put in your physical body has an effect on your mental state.

This is a connection that even mental health professionals often fail to make. As a result, most mental health professionals are treating symptoms instead of fixing the underlying problem; so even when people do seek help, they often don't get better.

Think of it this way: You break your leg, so you go to the

ER for help. Instead of taking an x-ray or examining the bone, the doctor asks you to describe your symptoms.

"What does your leg feel like?"

"Well, doctor," you say, "it hurts really bad."

"Where does it hurt?"

"Right here where the bone is broken."

"Can you walk on it?"

"No, I can't walk on it, and I'm in constant agony."

"Is this pain affecting your life?"

"Absolutely, doctor. I can barely get across my apartment, much less make it to class. I can't eat. I can't sleep. It's really terrible. My life is falling apart. Help me!"

After considering this a moment, the doctor replies, "Well, don't worry. We see a lot of cases just like yours. This sort of pain is normal, so we're just going to help you manage it. We'll give you some painkillers, do some physical therapy, and eventually you'll learn to live with your broken leg. In time, you'll have something approaching a normal life."

And before you know it, you're hopping out of the hospital on your broken leg with a prescription in your pocket.

That's a treatment plan that makes absolutely no sense, and you would never accept it. You would insist that the doctor fix the broken bone, treat the cause of the pain, and not just put you in a drugged stupor so you can endure it. If the doctor refused, you would get another doctor.

Something similar is happening in mental health care. People go in for help; doctors use their training to identify the symptoms a patient is experiencing and make a diagnosis aimed at managing those symptoms. Treatment is not about fixing the problem but about helping people learn to live with it.

SYMPTOMS ARE NOT THE ISSUE

The symptoms are not the issue. The symptoms, such as anxiety and depression, are merely expressions of the underlying cause. Since doctors often don't make the connection between mental and physical health, they typically suggest medication to help manage the symptoms, rather than helping patients fix the problem.

When I first began to struggle with anxiety and depression in college, I was reluctant to get help. After all, psychiatry is for crazy people, isn't it? It's something normal people don't do. The whole idea struck me as terrible and embarrassing. For a long time, this reluctance made me put off trying to get better.

Having finally gone down that road, I would first say that psychiatry should never be viewed as embarrassing. Seeking help for mental health problems is far more common than most people realize. At the same time, the way psychiatry is practiced these days simply doesn't work for most people.

Maybe, like me, you've been there. Maybe you're going through a mental health crisis right now. You've been to psychiatrists, you've been to therapists, and you've gotten various medications, but they simply haven't improved your quality of life. No matter what doctors give you to treat the symptoms, you aren't getting better. Is that your story?

Are you struggling to manage symptoms, but not healing? Maybe, like many people struggling with anxiety and depression, you simply feel lost. You have no hope that you'll ever be okay. Believe me, you're not alone.

Unfortunately, when mental health professionals fail to equip suffering people with the knowledge they need to fix their problems, they end up hurting their patients. In some cases, these people are hurt deeply. Perhaps you can relate. I know—I've been there.

The contrast between mental health care and other areas of medical practice is stark. Think about how far other areas of medical care have advanced in the last hundred years or so. Think about how much better doctors are at treating physical ailments.

It might be a bold statement, but I would say that mental health care has not only failed to advance but has in some ways gotten worse. Think about it. How many genuine mental health success stories have you heard? When is the last time you heard about someone going into a mental health facility and coming out cured?

"I'm a brand-new person! They fixed me!"

People do not leave mental health facilities healed. At best, they learn how to manage their symptoms better. In some cases, people wind up institutionalized for life, in and out of treatment, or pumped full of medication to the point that they can barely function.

Patients approach conventional treatment with a false sense of hope that their mental health problems can be cured; after all, doctors cure people, don't they? Instead, the patients become sicker, weaker, and even more anxious and depressed. Isn't it odd that one of the most common side effects of antianxiety medications is anxiety? Does that make any sense at all?

WHY COLLEGE STUDENTS?

Anxiety can happen to people at any age and in any stage of life, so why is it so common for college students? Why are so many college students struggling with mental health issues? I believe it's because college is a vulnerable time.

Prior to college, most young people live at home, so they have a support network of family and friends surrounding them all the time. This allows them to postpone dealing with their mental health problems and might event prevent the problems from developing in the first place. At the same time, they're busy most days, so it's easy to avoid having too many "alone" moments.

Suddenly, they go off to college, and their old support network is gone. They have newfound independence, and they're navigating a variety of new life challenges. It's easy for issues they've put off for years to suddenly manifest. Unfortunately, when that happens, most young adults lack both the tools to deal with these issues and the understanding to identify underlying causes.

At the same time, they are trying to figure out what they're going to do with their lives and how they're going to achieve their goals. This requires making some big decisions about careers, relationships, and personal pursuits.

That process is already stressful enough, and adding mental health problems only compounds the stress. Students seek treatment, and doctors throw potent medications into the mix. This creates tremendous suffering and affects not only the students' day-to-day lives but also all the decisions they're making about their futures.

Maybe that's where you are in your life right now. Maybe this is exactly what you've been going through. I want you to know there's hope.

THE WRONG TOOLS

I believe college students are being given the wrong tools to deal with their mental health problems. I get so sick of people being told that they simply have to manage the symptoms. That's a huge lie. In fact, it's the single biggest lie. If you're struggling with anxiety and depression, you don't need to manage your feelings. What you need are the tools that will actually bring about healing.

Part of the problem is that we live in a time when any deviation from normal health induces panic. If you wake up one day and don't feel as good as you did the day before, you assume that something terrible must be happening to you. Previous generations would have accepted the fact that some days people wake up and don't feel good. But now, we tend to panic. "Something is wrong with me! I must figure out what it is. Maybe I'm depressed. Maybe I have an anxiety disorder." We've become mental health hypochondriacs.

So what happens? Maybe you go online and start searching for your symptoms, trying to figure out what's wrong with you. Then you head to the psychiatrist to get help, and, invariably, the psychiatrist puts you on medication.

The psychiatric medications that people are commonly given typically only work for about a month, and they come with a laundry list of terrible side effects. They might take away your initial symptoms temporarily, but they aren't fixing the problem—and they're creating many new problems.

Mental health professionals either don't recognize or

don't emphasize the physical side of mental health. To be blunt, most psychiatrists are in the business of pushing medication, and pharmaceutical companies are in the business of making money. They visit a doctor's office and wine and dine the doctor, and soon the doctor is pushing their newest prescription drug. That's the business model.

In many instances, doctors have no idea if the medication they're pushing is safe or effective. They give it to patients, and occasionally they see those patients get a bit better. The truth is, they have no idea whether the improvement was the result of the medication or of something else entirely.

When college students struggle with mental health, they are led to believe that the problem is entirely in their own heads. It's a purely mental problem, and since there's no real cure, the message they receive is essentially: "Your life is going to be filled with anxiety and depression. That's just the way it's going to be. You will never be free of these things, so learn how to manage them."

Why don't people make the connection between their mental health and their physical health? Because they are never told about this connection. They have no idea that there are other solutions besides medication. Many people have never even considered the mind/body connection.

Society doesn't help. Unfortunately, society these days is really good at assigning labels, though it's often done in a way that sounds positive. "This is part of who you are. It's okay. There's nothing wrong with you." People are encouraged to take ownership of their mental health problems, but only to the extent of proudly embracing them.

Suppose a college student is struggling with depression. Maybe it's not severe depression that needs chemical intervention, but it's bad enough that she knows she needs some kind of help. What begins to happen is that she develops a strong sense of ownership over that depression.

"This is my depression. It's part of who I am, and it's okay. There's nothing wrong with who I am, and you're not taking my depression away from me."

She hates it, she hates how it makes her feel, but she embraces the fact that it's going to be there. It has become a part of her identity as a human being. Perhaps she doesn't want to let it go, because it's such a defining part of who she is.

That troubles me. So often, I want to tell people, "You don't have to live like this. It's not why you were put on this earth." Society shouldn't be okay with this. Why isn't there more significant interest in actually fixing the problem?

Instead of telling people to embrace their mental health problems, make them part of their identity, and learn to manage them, why aren't we teaching people how to heal? Listen, you can get rid of your anxiety! You can be free from depression! You can be rid of OCD, intrusive thoughts, and so many other mental health problems that people struggle with! Despite what you've been told, you don't have to carry these things around for the rest of your life.

THE HOW-TO COMPONENT

While books do exist that explain, mostly in vague terms, the connection between physical and mental health, what is lacking is a "how-to" component. "Here's how you can fix this, and here's why it works." That's the information that people need, and very little of that exists, especially from people who have successfully overcome such problems.

College students in particular need to understand that struggling with issues like anxiety and depression is common but not normal. They don't have to keep living the way they are living. Things can be much better. If you give the body what it wants, the body will heal itself.

Your lifestyle—what you're putting into your body, what you're doing, and what you're thinking about most of the day—is having an effect on your mental health. I say this from my own experience and research.

I suffered from severe anxiety during my college years. I had some difficult things going on in my life, but nothing I felt I couldn't handle, so the anxiety seemed to come out of nowhere. When I finally sought help, I went the traditional route. I tried therapy, I tried medication, I read everything I could find, and none of it worked. It didn't help me at all. On the contrary, the medications made me sicker. It was like putting poison into my body, and the doctors kept telling me I just had to learn how to manage my problems.

"Everybody deals with this. It's fine."

I never wanted to believe that. I didn't accept that my purpose on earth was to suffer every single day for my whole life. So, I changed my diet, added supplements, changed my sleeping habits, and experienced a miraculous healing. I changed every single thing about my physical health routine, and my life went back to normal.

I became anxiety-free. I simply gave my body what it wanted and was being deprived of. When I did that, it healed itself. Let me repeat that: my body completely healed itself.

This could be your story, too.

Chapter One

WHEN DISASTER STRIKES

———

Throughout my life, I've dealt with what I would call normal low-key anxiety, as everyone does. It never interfered with my life or took over, and it was always connected to identifiable causes.

When I was fourteen, I experienced sexual abuse at the hands of an older step-cousin. She had come to town over my birthday weekend. I was fourteen turning fifteen but had grown up in a sheltered environment. I attended a private Christian school, so I was never exposed to the harsh realities of the world. Internally, I was more like a ten-year-old, so, even though I knew that there was crazy stuff happening in the world, I had no real awareness of evil.

On top of that, my school had drilled into my head the idea that any type of sexual activity was sinful, and any kind of sin was a serious problem. Consequently, when I was abused, I did what many abused people do: I assumed it was my fault.

In fact, I went through six years of blaming myself: "I was a little bit curious, too, so even though she was older than me, it's not her fault. It's my fault for going along with it." I was convinced that I was a bad person because of this, and, as a result, anything sexual developed a negative connotation for me. I felt a tremendous amount of shame.

You might think that this was the moment when everything started to go wrong in my life, but initially, it wasn't a huge problem for me. It caused some anxiety, but I didn't go into a downward spiral. Overall, I had a fantastic life, and things were going along phenomenally. I had an amazing family who loved me very much.

Growing up, I was always busy and ambitious. At sixteen, I started flipping classic cars, buying and selling '70s Camaros. With the profits, I bought a race car and started racing competitively. While doing that, I got a job selling Cutco kitchen knives and did so well that I was promoted to manager in record time. In fact, I was the fastest-promoted salesperson in the office. I wound up running my own sales team and eventually took control of the entire sales office. My team experienced tremendous financial success, and I was constantly motivating them to do their best.

Everything seemed to be going great. When I graduated high school and went off to Arizona State University, I was excited. I loved everything about the experience, and I felt like I was truly in my element.

SUCCEEDING AT COLLEGE

I wasn't naïve about the dangers of going off to college. In high school, I had seen older kids leave for college and struggle. They were initially excited, but they never got involved in activities or made any new friends. Gradually, they started doing badly in classes, and eventually they dropped out or transferred to a different school.

Many of those people wound up in the local community college, living at home and commuting forty-five minutes to campus. There's nothing wrong with that, of course. It's possible to be completely successful doing that, but I didn't want to follow that path. I told myself, "If you're going off to college, you're going to succeed at it. You're going to make it work."

I chose Arizona State University in part because it was a long way from my home. This meant that when I arrived on campus, I only knew one person, so I was forced to get involved in activities to meet people. I wasted no time. As a freshman, I became president of an upperclassmen's sales organization. Most of the members had been involved for three years, and I became president after being involved for three weeks. I participated in a few other clubs as well and started making connections with professors in the business school. I made sure I didn't have any idle time. I was determined to be successful at college life.

THE DIAGNOSIS

While this was going on, back home my father was diagnosed with cancer. He received the diagnosis on September 2 of my freshman year. When they first called to tell me, I remember hearing the news and being underwhelmed. I was sitting at my desk drinking an Arizona Peach Tea, and though I teared up a little bit, my world wasn't rocked. I just went about my business. It didn't seem like a dire situation. Over the course of the school year, my parents withheld a lot of information from me. I don't blame them. They were scared to tell me what was really going on and just how serious it was.

My father had what's called GE junction cancer, which is a tumor where the esophagus meets the stomach. He went through chemo and radiation therapy for five weeks. The radiation was hardest on him. After a short time, it had agitated his esophagus so badly that he couldn't swallow. I remember visiting at one point and seeing him spitting into a cup because he couldn't even swallow his spit. In December, he underwent Ivor Lewis surgery, a procedure in which doctors removed two-thirds of his esophagus through his back, took out a large piece of his stomach, and performed what was essentially gastric-bypass surgery.

While they were doing the surgery, the doctors found another spot of cancer in his lung tissue. They told him about it after he had recovered slightly. Even though the tumor had been removed, he now faced more radiation, but he took it in stride. He maintained a positive attitude. I went to see him a few days after the surgery, and he was already walking around and trying to eat. The nurses complimented him for being such a great patient. I was amazed.

When they told him he needed more treatment, his response was, "No big deal. If it's what we have to do, I can handle it."

Forty-five days later, the cancer came back everywhere. It had spread over his entire body. He had twenty-five tumors in his abdomen. At this point, he was at stage four, and things weren't looking good. I, however, was back at Arizona State loving life and had no idea the cancer had come back so badly. During a meeting with one of his doctors at MD Anderson in Houston, my father was told bluntly: "With most cases like this, we'd say you've got a year and a half to live." My dad wouldn't accept it. He stopped seeing that doctor and went on a search for one who was interested in curing him, not managing him.

Through all of this, I really had no idea how bad things were. Since I wasn't around my parents and didn't see what was really going on, it didn't bother me all that much. Any time my dad called me, he sounded totally normal, so I assumed the best. My dad was always superhuman to me. He could handle anything.

In fact, on the phone, he sounded like the pinnacle of health. I went back home to visit a few times throughout the year, and each time I saw him, I would think, "Well, he's okay, but he's not great. He looks worse than he sounds—he's definitely sick." Still, it never seemed that serious to me.

Of course, my dad always held his head high. He endured

all his treatment with a positive attitude. "I'm going to beat this. I'm not going to die from this!" That's how he spoke to me, and that's how I assumed it was. I believed him.

MY WORLD IS ROCKED

I didn't learn different until I got home the following summer. The first two weeks back in my hometown were great. I had a lot of fun visiting friends and relaxing at home.

One night, we had a dinner party, and my parents invited a group of people to the house. Everyone was discussing my father's cancer, and I remember overhearing my mother say, "The first doctor told Jeff he had a year and a half to live."

When I heard that, I froze, thinking, "Wait a minute. What? You never told me they said you had a year and a half to live! I thought everything was going well."

Honestly, that one comment really shook me up. I had assumed my dad was getting close to remission. I thought the treatments were working, and the cancer was going away. He always sounded so confident. When I finally got the full story, I was shocked.

My younger sister handled it all a lot better than I did.

She was fourteen at the time and living at home, so she was there every day. It was like kids when they're growing up: the parents are around them all the time, so they don't realize how fast the kids are growing until other people come in town to visit and point it out: "Oh, my gosh, she's gotten so big!" My sister was in a similar situation. She saw my dad daily, so the changes in his health were gradual for her. For me, they were a surprise. I came home for the summer and suddenly discovered that my dad was dying.

Fortunately, he didn't die. On the contrary, he got a new doctor, and the treatment started working. Soon enough, he was on the road to recovery. In June, he got a clean bill of health. The doctor told him, "If we didn't have prior knowledge of your cancer, we would never know that you had been sick."

FEELING DISCONNECTED

My dad's recovery that summer was amazing. The strange thing about it was my reaction. Family friends, and even people I didn't know well, were weeping for joy at my dad's recovery. There was unbelievable excitement everywhere, and people were so happy. But for some reason, I didn't feel any of it.

I remember thinking, "It's really strange that I don't feel a huge sense of relief." I hardly felt anything at all. I excused it by saying, "Well, maybe it's because I always expected everything to turn out okay."

I never expected my dad to die. I had always assumed he was going to make it, so I never worried about him. Consequently, when he recovered, I didn't feel excited either. My dad was healthy. He was 100 percent cancer-free, and he was working every day again. He looked and felt fantastic.

What I know now is that this absence of emotion was actually self-preservation. The brain does this in an interesting way. We see it in abused children: they disconnect from the feeling of the abuse. In severe cases, they shut down and stop talking as a means of self-preservation. I think my brain did something similar on the day I learned my dad had cancer. It disconnected me emotionally from the situation.

THE CRASH

Because I was disconnected from the worry, I was also disconnected from the sense of excitement and relief at my dad's recovery. Things finally came crashing down for me one night when we were all together in the family room, watching *The Truman Show*. I remember lying on the couch, when intrusive thoughts suddenly started coming into my head.

For no apparent reason, my brain began telling me I was going to kill myself, I was going to hurt my girlfriend, I was going to do terrible things. I thought, "What the heck is going on right now?" And then I started feeling a terrible sense of anxiety in my chest. It felt like the sinking sensation that comes from being on an airplane that drops suddenly, but it didn't go away.

Finally, I spoke to my parents about this feeling, and somehow talking about it helped. I felt better the rest of the night. They comforted me.

"Listen, your dad is healed. He's fine. We're all good. There's nothing to be anxious about."

"Okay, you're right," I said. "I'm good."

But I woke up the next day and wasn't feeling healthy. I went shopping with my parents, and when we got to the store, I felt a sudden terrible panic. Standing there in the aisle, my body began screaming at me to run away, to flee, to escape. I tried to hold myself together as I turned to my parents and said, "I'm sorry. I have to get out of here.

We have to leave right now. I don't know what's wrong, but I do not feel good."

Concerned, they took me home right away, and I fell asleep on the couch, hoping that the feeling would pass. Unfortunately, I continued having similar episodes throughout the summer. Every day that summer, I woke up and instantly felt sick, both physically and mentally. I got into an unhealthy routine in which I walked downstairs in the morning, sat in a chair, and watched *The Office* for twelve hours straight, every single day—utterly paralyzed by anxiety, unable to go anywhere or do anything.

Now, as I mentioned, my parents were always positive people, especially my dad. My father founded a successful software company that is now worth billions of dollars. He's all about the power of positivity and being on top of the world. He's committed to a positive mindset. I have many childhood memories of getting into the car and hearing the harsh, raspy voice of Tony Robbins blasting out of the speakers as soon as my dad started the engine. He listened to those CDs all the time. I always quickly changed to a radio station.

Because he loved positivity, I did, too. When I worked at Cutco, I always strove to instill positivity in my team. I stressed the importance of bringing a positive mindset to everything they did. As a result, when I started experiencing daily anxiety, it was especially difficult for me, because I felt like I could no longer create or control my own happiness. For the first time in my life, I was depressed, and I couldn't overcome the depression with positivity. Nothing I did eliminated the negative feelings, and I had no control over my own happiness. That was extremely hard to accept.

I had always been against therapy. That stuff was for crazy people, or so I thought. But finally, I knew I had to do something, so I started seeing a therapist. Unfortunately, that first therapist was terrible. The good things she said didn't help, and the bad things she said were very hurtful.

One day, she asked me, "What does it feel like to have anxiety? Describe it to me. Personally, I've never felt anxiety. I've only heard about it from my clients."

I remember thinking, "What the heck is wrong with you? You've never felt anxiety? How can you provide therapy for anxiety if you don't know what it feels like?" First, she was lying. Everybody feels anxiety at some point in their lives. Second, that's a horrible thing to say to a patient: it makes them feel worse about themselves.

The therapist didn't help me, and the anxiety was interfering with my life more and more, so finally she recommended medication. I was torn. On the one hand, I thought, "This is good. Maybe meds will fix the problem." On the other hand, I had always looked down on the idea that people needed medication for emotional problems. Suddenly, it was going to be me taking meds. I was torn between outrage and relief.

CHIHUAHUAS IN THE ROOM

The therapist eventually sent me to one of the best psychiatrists in Dallas. I remember sitting in the waiting room. I had come directly from a speaking engagement, so I was wearing a nice suit. I'd been invited to guest-speak at a Cutco office and teach their team different sales techniques. Generally, I was very good at turning my professional persona on and off throughout these struggles. Whenever I needed to be on point, I could act normal, and people never suspected a thing.

When I walked into the waiting room, I knew I needed to switch off the professional persona and deal with the problems I was putting on hold. I walked in thinking, "I feel fine. What am I doing here?"

The psychiatrist turned out to be a fantastic doctor and incredible person, but unfortunately, he was stuck in the old ways and didn't look at the whole person.

I told him what was going on. I talked about the anxiety, the intrusive thoughts about hurting myself and loved ones. I told him everything. His response was surprisingly nonchalant, which actually gave me a temporary sense of relief.

"Okay, you're going to be just fine," he said. "You're going to be totally okay. I want you to understand that there's nothing wrong with you. You're having some bad thoughts, and you're anxious, and that's normal. Evan, people obsess about their thoughts, and that's what you're doing. You're making them a bigger problem than they really are."

He told me to imagine that there were two Chihuahuas running around the office. Then he asked me, "Wouldn't that be strange?"

"Yes," I admitted. "That would be very weird."

"But it wouldn't interrupt our conversation," he said. "Would it? We would let the dogs run around, and we would observe them, and we would say, 'Wow, how interesting that these two little dogs are in the room. I wonder what they're doing here.' But it wouldn't interrupt us or prevent us from talking to each other."

He said my intrusive thoughts were like those little Chihuahuas running around in my head.

"This is what you're dealing with," he said. "Because these are your thoughts, you can let them dance around in your head. It's only when you attach meaning to them that they become a problem. When you take a thought that you know isn't you, and you say, 'Why am I thinking that? Does it make me a bad person?'—that's where you go wrong. You can have bad thoughts, but you have to ignore them like crazy. You have to ignore the heck out of them."

At the end of the meeting, he said, "I'm going to give you something to calm the thoughts down, but you're going to be okay." I was prescribed Zoloft, also known as sertraline, a common medication that many people take.

MEDICATED

The next morning, my dad woke me up early so I could run an errand with him. He was a fantastic, supportive person through all of this, but he was still worried about me. He always wanted me to be as happy as possible.

His way of helping was to try to keep me doing things that I would normally do. He packed me in the car that morning, and we drove downtown to shop for a suit, which was one of my favorite things to do. The whole way there, I hung my head. I felt sick, and I remember thinking, "This is the worst thing ever. I didn't know it was possible to feel this bad." It was the first day I was supposed to start taking Zoloft, but I hadn't taken it yet. The pill was in my pocket.

On the way, my father insisted we stop at a grocery store to get something to eat. I didn't want to go in. I didn't want to eat, but I also didn't care. I was on autopilot, so I wasn't even interested in stating an opinion.

The grocery store had a little deli counter, and I selected a fruit tray. It seemed like something I should be able to eat—an easy meal—even in my anxious condition.

We sat down at a table in a back corner, and I put the tray in front of me. It had four slices of watermelon, a little scoop of vanilla yogurt, and some blueberries, and I couldn't even eat half of it. I sat staring at the tray of food, thinking, "I used to be able to eat so much food. Why can't I do that anymore? What is causing this loss of appetite?" I was already noticeably losing weight. In fact, I looked somewhat sickly. I just couldn't force the food down.

After throwing away the uneaten portion, we got back in the car and continued downtown. I still had the Zoloft pill and was rolling it around in my hand. My dad and I didn't speak. I couldn't say anything. I put my head in my left hand, the pill in my right hand, and for forty-five minutes, as we drove, I contemplated taking it. I knew that once I swallowed that pill, I had crossed the line. At that point, I would go from "I'm fighting" to "I'm medicated." As soon as I took the pill, it would become a part of my life.

We arrived at the clothing store and walked in. My dad's favorite suit salesman, Zack, was standing there with a big smile on his face and said, "Hey, how are you doing, Mr. York?" Then he turned and greeted me in his great big, gregarious way. He was so upbeat, so happy to see us. We began picking out clothes and looking at shoes, and I started to feel better.

There came a point when I suddenly felt good. I had reached some semblance of normal, and I thought, "This is my chance. I'll take the pill now while I have the will-power to do it." So I took it. I didn't even think about it. Mid-conversation with Zack, I popped the Zoloft in my mouth and swallowed it, and that was that.

The doctor had started me on 50 milligrams of Zoloft with plans to move up to 100 milligrams after a week.

SICKER AND SICKER

The day after my dad and I went shopping, my whole family went to dinner with some friends. On the way to their house, I was suddenly overwhelmed with nausea.

I'd always been a healthy person; in fact, I hadn't thrown up since I was three years old. I rarely feel nausea, but this hit me hard.

My parents asked if I wanted to go back home, but, not wanting to spoil the evening, I said no. We showed up at our friends' house, and I tried my best to act normal. Everyone was talking, hanging out, and having a good time, but I just felt sick.

Ultimately, I found myself sitting in a chair in the family's living room, and I stayed there the whole night, doing nothing. I didn't go to the dinner table. I didn't eat or drink anything. Even the smell of food was too much. Instead, I just sat, feeling sick and waiting for the night to end, so I could go home and climb into bed.

When I told my doctor about this, he lowered my dosage from 50 to 25 milligrams. He said my body needed to become more accustomed to the drug. The side effects went away, and for a while I felt okay. The anxiety and intrusive thoughts were still there, but they were not as strong. Looking back, I now believe these improvements were merely a placebo effect.

Since my problems weren't going away, the doctor eventually upped my dosage again. I went from twenty-five to fifty, then fifty to seventy-five, and finally seventy-five to one hundred milligrams. By that point, the medication was wreaking havoc on my body. I had diarrhea every day, all day, for months.

I also became severely hypoglycemic. If I didn't eat within five minutes of waking up, my blood sugar would crash, and my whole day would be ruined. If I didn't eat every hour or so, I would feel miserable the rest of the day.

I was sleeping terribly every single night. I would wake up at three o'clock in the morning, drenched in sweat, and try to force myself to go back to bed. Through all of this, I was told, "Oh, these are just common side effects. They're bound to happen. But would you rather have the side effects or feel the terrible anxiety?"

"Actually, I'd rather feel normal again," I thought.

I went through months of waking up at three in the morning, lying in a puddle of sweat, and feeling a tingling sensation all over my body. This became my life and daily routine, and it was hell. Everything was going haywire.

I went back to college, and my mental health crisis continued. I had no idea what to do. I was on medication, I was in therapy, and nothing was working. I knew there had to be something better out there. This wasn't the way I was meant to live the rest of my life.

It became my mission to figure out what was making me sick, and once I did, I was going to share it with the rest of the world.

So that's exactly what I did.

Chapter Two

SOUND FAMILIAR?

Let's examine some of the common mental health symptoms that people deal with. I want you to think whether these descriptions seem familiar to you. Is what you're going through normal?

ANXIETY

Natural anxiety is something everybody experiences. It's the "fight or flight" response, the adrenaline reaction. It's also situational. Basically, when you get into a difficult situation, your brain tells your body to release stress hormones—adrenaline and cortisol—which elevate your heart rate. You then either get away from the situation, or you fight it. Whether you're speaking on stage in front of a crowd, taking an important test, or coming face-to-face with a rattlesnake, natural anxiety is a common response: it's normal.

Unexplained anxiety is something different. This is the kind of anxiety that comes out of nowhere. You might have a few things in your life that are stressing you out, maybe projects at school or work, but none of it is serious or tearing your life apart. You feel anxiety anyway. You feel the fight-or-flight response, but it's not connected to anything in particular. There doesn't seem to be an actual cause.

This is exactly what happened to me that first night on the couch, watching *The Truman Show*. I was in the most dormant state possible, lying on a couch, watching a movie. It should have been a relaxing moment, but instead I felt wound up like a top. My body was having a reaction that would have been useful if I had needed to run away from someone who was trying to kill me. But I had no reason to feel that way: there was no immediate threat.

Natural anxiety is a survival mechanism. Without it, we wouldn't survive as individuals or as a species. This is not the case with unexplained anxiety. What I felt on the couch that night was, ultimately, a serious waste of energy; it was my body malfunctioning. I had no reason to feel that way. This kind of anxiety is abnormal, but it's also quite common.

Too many people who experience unexplained anxiety assume they have to live with it. Sometime later, I was working as an administrative assistant at the Arizona State University Counseling Services Center, and one day I asked my boss, "What do you guys do here? What's your purpose? What's your mission?"

She considered my questions and replied, "Well, what we really want to do is equip students with the tools to manage their anxiety and depression and let them know that it's okay to feel that way. It's normal, and with the tools we give them, they can still live a very normal life. They are simply learning how to manage their own brains."

She went on to talk about something else, but I stopped there, thinking about her answer. Finally, the conversation circled back, and I had to say something.

"When a psychiatrist, psychologist, or any kind of medical professional tells a patient that they simply have to manage their anxiety and live with it for the rest of their lives, I think that is the single biggest lie that is being told."

She looked at me with surprise, but all she said was, "Mm-hmm."

I was surprised myself. Had I really said that to my boss?

This woman had devoted her entire life to this practice, and I was telling her it was invalid.

Even realizing what I'd said, I didn't take it back. I didn't regret saying it, because, in the end, I was angry that this organization was centered around telling students that they simply had to learn to live with anxiety and depression, that all they could hope for was a way to manage these things.

"That's no way to live," I went on. "That's no way to live! If I believed I was put on this earth to live a life filled with daily stress and anxiety and depression, then, quite frankly, I wouldn't want to live here."

"Furthermore," I added, "as a man of faith, if I believed that the God I worship put me on this earth simply to suffer like that for the rest of my life, then I would want nothing to do with that faith."

It was an uncomfortable moment for her, I'm sure. I concluded by saying, "There are people here who are telling serious lies! Anxiety and depression can be fixed. They aren't terrible burdens that people have to carry for the rest of their lives. People need real hope. They need to be told they can find true healing. I'm convinced that human beings are meant to flourish on this earth."

At this point, my boss made no attempt to defend herself. She didn't say anything. She just looked at me, smiled, and nodded. I like to think I sparked a thought in her that day. I hope I did.

DEPRESSION

As with anxiety, there are two kinds of depression. One of them is normal, and the other is not. Normal, explainable depression is circumstantial. When a loved one dies, you go through a natural grieving process. We all experience circumstantial depression: it's part of what makes us human.

This isn't news to anyone. We know and expect that when sad things happen to us, we will feel sad. If we lose a job, a pet, or an important personal possession, we expect to have an emotional response as part of coming to terms with the loss. In all of these situations, there is an explanation for our emotions.

However, there is also a type of depression that is inexplicable. It's a chronic, free-floating emotion that lingers in the back of the sufferer's head. If you suffer from chronic depression, you wake up feeling like a weight has been laid on your body, and you don't know why. You're not upset about anything in particular. You have nothing to grieve for, but the feeling remains.

As with unexplained anxiety, the body is malfunctioning. We're not supposed to feel this way, and most people understand this when it happens. We have all heard about, or even experienced, this kind of inexplicable depression. What many people don't realize, or don't accept, is that the feeling is not all in the mind. It's not simply the result of faulty thoughts. It is due to something physical and tangible in the body that can be fixed.

Chronic depression is not so much about mental health as it is about brain health. Yes, there's a difference, which we'll get to a little later. My depression was both. Some of it stemmed from my dad's diagnosis, but much of it was not connected to anything, a free-floating emotion with no cause. I felt depressed every day and had no idea why. Does that sound familiar to you?

OCD

When most people think of obsessive-compulsive disorder (OCD), they think about some poor kid washing his hands six times every minute or walking circles in front of the kitchen sink. Although those kinds of things do happen, OCD is actually a more generalized condition.

There are many different types of OCD. Some are primarily external, while others are internal. However, what the term ultimately refers to is any sort of obsession that leads to compulsive behavior. Pure-O (or Pure Obsessional) OCD is inward and blends with intrusive thoughts. It's what I was experiencing, as a lot of other people have.

This typically manifests as a thought that sufferers can't let go of. When a person has Pure-O OCD, a specific thought keeps racing through their heads. They dissect it and play it over and over again in a loop, and it begins to overwhelm them. Eventually, they start to question their own sanity.

"What is wrong with me? Am I schizophrenic?"

Still, they can't shake the thought. They start to panic, so they do what so many people do: they hop on the Internet and start searching for every symptom of schizophrenia. They just want to make sure they don't have it. They search for every possible mental health problem, trying to diagnose themselves and make sure they aren't losing their minds.

This is endless and can run somebody's life. I know this all too well.

INTRUSIVE THOUGHTS

Everybody has intrusive thoughts from time to time.

You've probably experienced them—thoughts that fly into your brain out of nowhere, leaving you wondering, "Why the heck did I just think that?" The thoughts might be particularly sick or disturbing but, if you're like most people, you find that they soon go away, allowing you to move on with your day.

One out of every fifty people, however, will attach a meaning to these intrusive thoughts and begin to wonder, "Am I a bad person for thinking about this? Is something wrong with me?"

Where do intrusive thoughts come from? Often, they are influenced by the media and what's going on in society. For example, back in the 1980s, a lot of intrusive thoughts were influenced by media coverage of the AIDS epidemic. People were paranoid about contracting AIDS.

If such people touched a doorknob, they might think, "Oh, that doorknob has AIDS. I'd better wash my hands a million times." Or they might meet someone and think, "Uh oh, what if that person has AIDS? What if I shake hands with him and catch the disease?"

Nowadays, intrusive thoughts tend to be violent, because so many media stories are about violent events. Parents may have intrusive thoughts about harming or abusing their own children. In reality, they're normal people, but they experience terrible thoughts about killing loved ones. This sounds gruesome, but it's simply their fears being shaped in a particular way.

In fact, if you struggle with intrusive thoughts, you'll often find that they are associated with the things you fear the most. What does every parent fear above almost anything else? Their child being sexually abused or physically harmed.

The problem is that your brain doesn't know the difference between you and the TV. The brain is an incredible instrument, but it can also be obtuse. When it takes in negative images, it can't differentiate between that external image and the internal person. That means that, when you hear media reports about mass shootings or violent crimes, your brain puts you behind the gun. You are now playing out this role in your head. You are the person committing the crime.[1]

Your intrusive thoughts make you the shooter, the person abusing children, the terrible person doing terrible things. The news media has subconsciously altered your brain into thinking that these stories have happened to you. Recognizing that should alleviate some of the stress.

---

1   See Intrusive Thoughts, accessed August 11, 2017, https://www.intrusivethoughts.org.

The brain reacts to intrusive thoughts in one of two ways. In most cases, the prefrontal cortex, which is the decision-making part of your brain, helps you dismiss them. Maybe you have an intrusive thought, for example, about robbing a convenience store at gunpoint. The prefrontal cortex kicks in and says, "Well, if I did that, I would go to prison for the rest of my life, and I wouldn't be able to spend time with my family. Of course I'm not going to shoot up a convenience store. It's not an option." This doesn't actually play out as a conversation in your head, because it happens in a fraction of a second.

However, one in fifty people who experience intrusive thoughts will begin to question themselves. "Could I really do that? Could I actually be that kind of person? Maybe this is who I really am!"

My own intrusive thoughts were really dark and made me question myself. "Could I hurt somebody that I love? Could I hurt myself? Do I actually want to do that?"

I began to question my own integrity, and it became an endless, horrible game in my head. The thoughts started to wedge themselves in between my normal self and the fiction my brain was spinning.

THE CAUSES

Anxiety, depression, OCD, intrusive thoughts—what causes these kinds of problems? Believe it or not, the answer is neither mystical nor impossible to figure out. These symptoms have many causes. Perhaps you've experienced trauma that you've never dealt with. Because you've never dealt with it, your subconscious is triggered on a daily basis as you encounter things that remind you of the trauma.

I believe that for me one cause was the sexual abuse I experienced at age fourteen. I'd never dealt with the abuse. Any time I was in a sexual situation, or even thought about or overheard someone talking about a sexual experience, I was immediately brought back to that time and the shame and anxiety it produced. I needed to deal with that trauma in order to move on, but I didn't want to talk to anyone about it.

Other causes of these symptoms are primarily physical. This is what many people don't understand, and it's the main point and purpose of sharing my story. What happens to your body affects your mental health. I'll give you an example. The primary food source for your brain is glucose. It's a type of sugar, but it's neither the processed stuff you may think of when you think of sugar, nor fructose, the sugar you find in fruit.

When your blood sugar gets low, your brain is essentially starved of its food source, so your body triggers a state of emergency. Since your brain is running low on fuel, your "low gas" light turns on, and your body starts to freak out.

What happens at that point feels a lot like being chased by a lion. Your body dumps stress hormones into your system. It dumps adrenaline and cortisol, because that's the body's natural response to an emergency. All your body knows is that there's danger, and that you need to get away from it.

Your body experiences the fight-or-flight sensation, which sends you into full-fledged panic mode. But there's no lion. You have nothing to run away from. In all likelihood, you're just typing at your computer, and the real cause of the sensation is that your blood sugar, your glucose, is too low. A physical problem is affecting your mental state.

Unattended brain health problems can also cause these symptoms. There have been cases in which violent people were found to have cysts in their brains. The cysts were causing the brain to malfunction, producing high levels of aggression. Once removed, the individuals' behavior went back to baseline.

Traumatic brain injuries, like concussions, or circulatory problems in the brain can also contribute to anxiety, depression, OCD, and intrusive thoughts. What I want you to see is that the feelings are neither merely symptoms of physical problems nor the problem themselves. The root cause—the injury, the cyst, the low blood sugar—needs to be addressed.

When something physical is malfunctioning in your body, treating the symptoms won't fix it. If you want to heal, the source of the malfunction must be dealt with. In a few instances—a very, very select few—people who are experiencing these kinds of mental health symptoms really do have severe problems, such as severe bipolar disorder, schizophrenia, or both, which require more intensive treatment, as well as the remedies we're going to explore in this book.

Feeling bad is something different than these kinds of severe mental health problems, however, and does not require medication. You may have psychiatrists poking and prodding you, but you just need to get your body back to normal. Your mental health symptoms might be linked to trauma, but they are often linked to—and made worse by—the brain's and body's malfunctioning.

What do you need to do to get better? Let's find out.

Chapter Three

"TAKE TWO AND CALL ME IN THE MORNING"

———

Some mental health problems can't be addressed through the mind/body connection alone. There are symptoms that require immediate medical intervention, and in those cases, the things I'll outline in this book aren't what are needed immediately.

If you're having suicidal thoughts because of lingering anxiety and depression, this book is for you. It can help improve your situation. However, if you've reached the point where you've made a plan for how you're going to kill yourself, or if you're planning on doing it soon, then you need immediate, emergency intervention. Put down this book, and go get help! Don't wait a minute longer.

Once things are better, you can come back and put these things into practice for long-term help to improve your life.

The same goes for homicidal thoughts and self-harm. If there is immediate danger, you need critical care. Don't put it off.

The mental health problems I'm addressing in this book can be treated and even eliminated, but this rarely happens through traditional psychiatric care. Notice I said "eliminated," not "managed." Yes, it's possible to eliminate anxiety, depression, OCD, and intrusive thoughts completely. Nevertheless, many people never find freedom. They endure years of misery and finally give up hope.

I have a good friend who is going through exactly what I went through. He struggles with anxiety and depression daily, and nothing that he's tried thus far has helped. Unfortunately, he's reached a point where he doesn't even want to deal with his problems, because he feels that the sheer amount of information about mental health problems is too overwhelming. He gets frustrated trying to navigate all the options.

Though he's seen the change in my life, he's not yet convinced that what I've done will work for him. He's gotten his hopes up too many times in the past, and he's lost his will to try. Instead, he spends each day trying to get by as best he can, unhappy and barely hanging on.

Although I continue to encourage him and provide support, I understand the mounting frustration that comes from trying to find the right solution. There is, indeed, an overwhelming amount of information out there.

In the waiting room of the counseling center at Arizona State University, there's a huge array of dozens of different pamphlets covering a dizzying number of mental health problems. One day, I stood staring at all these pamphlets and thought, "How could a suffering student possibly tell the difference between multiple types of depression or multiple types of anxiety? Someone who is miserable and hopeless is going to feel lost staring at this display. They won't even know where to start."

In the world of mental health care, there is way too much material—from pamphlets to books to webpages—to wade through. At the same time, there's little that is tailored specifically to young adults and college students. As in my friend's case, the combination of the two can cause many people simply to give up.

Another contributing factor is the lack of results. Most of the time, sick people look at those who have gone through psychiatric treatment and don't see much improvement. Rarely do people come out of treatment saying, "Yeah, I had mental health struggles, but I'm now healed. All of the pain and suffering is gone. I'm cured!"

Instead, what they usually say is something like: "I've had mental health struggles, but I'm on a really good run of medication, and now I can manage things better. I don't feel great, but I don't feel quite as awful as I did before. I'm in a good place." That is not what I call healing.

I don't blame people for giving up. It takes a great deal of perseverance to push through all the noise and confusion to find healing. When you don't feel good, that perseverance can be hard to dredge up. In the midst of my crisis, I had days when it took all my energy just to get out of bed.

In the end, I was lucky, because I'm unusually tenacious. I wouldn't accept half answers, terrible side effects, or guesswork. Throughout my crisis, I was determined to figure out exactly what was wrong with me and how to fix it. Fortunately, I encountered the right people along the way and got better. Some are not so lucky.

STUCK IN THE 1950S

The first antidepressant drug, Chlorpromazine, came out

in the 1950s, and since then, no new medication has been more effective. The same is true of lithium, which doctors have used for decades to treat bipolar disorder. To this day, there is no more effective treatment. It seems that the only thing that has changed is the increase in the severity of the side effects of the drugs that have come out since.

Unlike other medical fields, psychiatric treatment hasn't seen improvement. If anything, it's falling farther behind, as the percentage of Americans with disabling mental illness has increased fivefold. The drug-centered paradigm of care simply isn't working. In many instances, it makes people worse. The research speaks for itself.[1]

What are we doing? What is the point of all of this? Doctors are stuck with an antiquated Freudian mentality, uncovering early childhood causes of adult problems, but the response to almost every situation is medication, more medication, or different medication. Doctors want to whip up a special cocktail of drugs that's going to fix all of their patients' problems.

"Take this pill for intrusive thoughts. Take this pill for depression. Here's one for anxiety. And, finally, here's

---

1   See Robert Whitaker, "Anatomy of an Epidemic: Psychiatric Drugs and the Astonishing Rise of Mental Illness in America," Ethical Human Sciences and Services 7, no. 1 (2005): 23–35, http://www.ingentaconnect.com/content/springer/ehss/2005/00000007/00000001/art00003.

another one just because. Let's see if these make you feel better."

In most fields, doctors look for actual problems and root causes. Orthopedic doctors, for example, examine bones, looking for damage and making sure the bones are healthy. Cardiologists look at the heart. They scan and examine it to discover problems, which they then address. Neurologists do the same with the brain. They look for physical problems in the organ so they can treat them. In most fields of medical practice, doctors look at scans to find tangible problems in bodily systems.

Psychiatrists, on the other hand, listen to patients describe their symptoms and then make educated guesses at what might be wrong. Based on those guesses, they prescribe medications that might work to address the guessed-at problems, and then they wait to see what happens. If the results are calamitous, they typically respond by switching to another medication and trying again.

They're trying to heal the organ that runs the entire body, and they're running on guesswork. Let me repeat that: they're guessing about treatment for the organ that runs the entire body. That's a real problem.

I can't shake the feeling that most mental health professionals have simply lost touch. Suppose your dog gets sick or isn't acting right, and you take it to the vet. The first question the vet is going to ask you is, "What have you been feeding your dog?" It's the first potential problem they're going to look for.

Why? Because veterinarians know that if you give dogs the wrong food, they aren't going to function properly. If, for example, you give dogs cat food, they are going to get sick, and that illness will be reflected in their behavior. Cat food is not what their bodies need, and their bodies are going to make sure they know it.

In the same way, if you put the wrong kind of fuel into a car, it's going to break down. At the very least, it isn't going to work properly. If you put too much voltage into a light bulb, it's going to explode. If you put too little, it won't light up. Since these connections exist everywhere else, why don't we make them in mental health?

Humans have decided to override the evolutionary process in regard to what we eat and drink. We've transformed our diets in half a century, so now we're filling ourselves with processed, unnatural foods and beverages. We create these foods in labs and consume them, whether our bodies are adapted to them or not, assuming everything is going to be okay.

AGGRESSION

A man named Dr. Daniel Amen wound up having a tremendous impact on my life. I'll speak about him later, but for now, I want to talk about his nephew. You see, he had a young nephew who became violent. The nephew started drawing awful pictures at school: images of himself shooting other children or hanging himself. Finally, the violence in the drawings bled over into real life. One day, he attacked a girl on a baseball field in a park for no reason. He just ran up and lashed out at her.

Most doctors were ready to medicate him. They figured he needed drugs to calm him down and bring him back to normal. Dr. Amen decided to scan his brain instead. He used what's called a SPECT scan and discovered a cyst in the child's brain. SPECT scans look at blood flow and other activity in the brain, giving a clear picture of which parts are functioning properly or not. This allows the select few doctors who use these scans to treat patients based on what's actually happening instead of guessing. No amount of medication would have fixed this child's problem. He needed surgery to remove the cyst. Masking the symptoms with meds would never have cured him.

Once the cyst was removed, the nephew's behavior went back to normal. All his violent tendencies disappeared, and he was 100 percent better. The change was immediate. Why? Because the physical cause of his problem had been dealt with. His story makes me wonder about some of the mass shootings that have become so common in the United States. Is it possible that some of the perpetrators, rather than simply being terrible human beings, had something physically wrong with their brains? Absolutely.

On the university campus, I see so many students going to the doctor, complaining about an inability to concentrate. The students are given prescriptions and end up abusing stimulants. Eventually, they feel like they need the drugs.

"I just can't focus without the drugs," they say. "I can't do my homework. I can't pay attention in class."

College is supposed to be the time of their lives. Their brains aren't even finished forming yet, and now they're introducing something that is altering the brain chemically.

This is not limited to college students. People of all ages, even older adults, particularly women, are going to the doctor these days, saying, "I feel so tired all the time. I'm fatigued. I can't get anything done. Help me." They walk out five minutes later with an antianxiety or antidepressant prescription. Diet and exercise are rarely, if ever, addressed. What a horrible way to care for people!

TWO PATHS

I have an acquaintance who has dealt with anxiety and depression for years, but he's no longer looking for a solution. Instead, he has accepted that these feelings are an essential part of his identity as a person.

"This is who I am. This is what I struggle with. This is me."

He takes medication, he experiences all the unpleasant side effects, he continues to struggle every single day with the symptoms and side effects, and that's it. That is his life, and he's resigned himself to it.

Another buddy of mine lost himself for a while in the world of mental health care. As a teenager living in Detroit, he was surrounded by friends who were bad influences. They got him smoking weed every day, drinking, and skipping class. It affected his grades and mood, and he started butting heads with his teachers. He seemed to be on a downward spiral.

Finally, he decided, "I'm not going to live this way. This lifestyle doesn't make me happy, so I'm going to change things." Since he didn't know any other way to break free of the negative influences around him, he ran away from home at the age of fifteen.

Understandably, his parents were distraught. They tracked

him down and brought him home. Concerned about his behavior and change of mood, they had him admitted to a mental hospital.

The young man was convinced he wasn't crazy. Yes, his mood had changed, and his behavior had changed along with it, but from his perspective, he was only trying to find his way and making some mistakes. Once he was institutionalized, however, doctors immediately tried to put him on psychiatric medication.

Afraid to lose himself in a fog of prescription drugs, he refused to take the pills, so doctors switched to injections. These transformed him completely. His personality sank into a medicated mire, and he turned into an emotionless zombie, a shell of his former self.

He wound up in and out of the hospital three times, as doctors struggled to find the right drug cocktail for him. When his treatment finally ended, he decided to get off the medication and get healthy again. He wanted to find his way back to normal, so he researched, studied, and began to make changes to his lifestyle.

Through this research, and by making environmental and emotional changes, he brought his life back on the right track. Now, he's working to help others. He's doing groundbreaking research on addiction therapy, and he reaches out to other people who are going through similar experiences.

So we have two young people struggling with mental health who wound up taking wildly different paths. One embraced the belief that he would never get better, accepted that he would be medicated for the rest of his life, and resigned himself to the side effects. The other saw what the medication did to him and successfully devoted his life to finding a better way.

Too many people choose the former path, allowing themselves to become victims of their symptoms and side effects.

What about you?

THE STIGMA OF THERAPY

When I was growing up, I knew a few people who went to therapy for what I considered to be legitimate reasons—for example, childhood friends dealing with the divorce of their parents. I understood why they might need to talk through their feelings with a professional. However, in most cases, I viewed therapy as something primarily for crazy people. Who speaks to a therapist because they feel anxious or depressed? That was my attitude even when my own symptoms began to manifest, and I've met others who share that feeling.

In general, frat boys on college campuses don't roll into counseling services looking for help. People don't bring it up in class. "Hey, by the way, I went to the therapist today, and it was great." It's rarely talked about in public, because it's seen as embarrassing and makes people feel vulnerable. Mental health care is viewed as a secretive thing that must, at all costs, be kept private.

Those fears are not entirely unfounded. There is definitely a stigma attached to therapy, especially for young adults, who can be intensely concerned with how others perceive them.

Of course, there's nothing to be embarrassed about. Having mental health problems is no different than breaking a limb, catching the flu, or having an allergic reaction. In other words, it's just another example of the body malfunctioning and needing to be fixed. Seeking help is the logical response.

In my experience, talking to a skilled professional can be tremendously helpful. My first therapist was a disaster. She said some things that made me feel worse, and she ultimately set me on a path that increased my suffering immensely.

However, I later found a second therapist who was her polar opposite. The second therapist brought a lot of compassion and wisdom to the table. From the beginning, she was thoughtful and considerate, and she knew how to respond to my concerns. Meeting with her was helpful, since it allowed me to talk through a lot of confusion and put things into perspective. I still meet with her today, as it's helpful to run things by a professional for an outside perspective.

College students need to hear that, if they are having emotional problems, they have nothing to feel ashamed of. Whatever they're going through or whatever their mental health symptoms might be, they are not alone. Countless others have gone through the same things.

This highlights another tragic consequence of the secretive way most of us treat mental health problems; people never realize just how many others are going through the same thing. They see their peers and think, "Wow, all these other people are normal, and here I am, falling apart," when nothing could be further from the truth.

A BETTER WAY

If people are seeking help, they need a cure. So, the question remains: Is there a better way than psychiatric medication to treat, even cure, mental health problems? Is it possible that people can do more than mask symptoms? Can they actually get better?

Yes, I firmly believe so. The first step, as I've mentioned, is to realize the connection between brain health and physical health. Most people don't understand this, simply because they've never been told. In fact, I'd never have made the connection until I saw it with my own eyes.

This began one day when I was driving home from class. Suddenly, I started feeling that all-too-familiar anxiety, the sinking sensation that doesn't go away, the cold sweat and racing heart. I felt as if I hadn't slept in days.

After a little while, the symptoms went away on their own. The whole episode came and went without any clear cause. The next time I met with my therapist, I described the incident at length.

She listened, considered for a moment, and said, "Evan, do these episodes happen frequently?"

"Yes," I replied.

"Do they tend to happen at the same time of the day?

I thought about it and realized that they did.

"You know what? They do tend to happen at the same time. Around five o'clock. All of a sudden, for no particular reason, this feeling just sweeps over me, and I feel completely wiped out and ready to collapse in my bed, even if it hasn't been a hard day. Then, after a little while, the feeling just sort of goes away, and I pick back up again."

"Do you ever feel sick when you wake up in the morning?" she asked.

"Yes," I replied. "I feel sick the second I open my eyes."

"How often?"

"Every single morning," I said. "It's my daily routine. I can't remember the last time I woke up and felt normal."

She nodded and said, "I wonder if you're hypoglycemic."

I knew what hypoglycemia was, but I'd never thought it was something I suffered from, because I'm not diabetic. I had no idea it might be connected to the way my brain felt. I'd assumed I was completely breaking down. Until my therapist mentioned it, I had no idea there might be a simple problem behind these awful episodes.

"I think your blood sugar is dropping," she said. "It might be affecting you mentally."

For the first time, a mental health professional was telling me that what I was feeling wasn't all in my head, that it might have something to do with my body as well.

"Look," she said. "You are not just your mind. You are comprised of your mind, your body, and your spiritual side. All of these things combined create the person we call Evan. You have to examine everything to locate the cause."

After that meeting, I went directly to the store and bought a blood glucose meter, the same device a diabetic would use. A couple of days later, I went to have some clothes tailored, and on my way home, I started feeling anxiety again, that sinking sensation with nervousness and trembling. I got home and walked upstairs, intending to get some food, but decided to test my blood sugar first. I remember that moment like it was yesterday. Standing there in the bathroom, staring at the glucose meter, I saw the number come up, and, lo and behold, it was twenty points below what is considered the low end of normal.

e actual number was 50 mg/dl, which is low enough that health-care professionals consider it dangerous. I stared at the number, and it was a huge revelation for me. Here was proof of an actual physical problem in my body that was causing me to experience these terrible episodes. What was happening in my body was directly affecting what was going on in my mind!

That moment was a breakthrough for me. I had never considered the possibility that my emotional problems might be a direct result of the kinds of foods I was putting, or failing to put, into my body.

It makes sense, but I had to hear it from a professional to grasp it. If you put bad fuel into your body, you're putting bad fuel into your brain. If you don't put enough of the right fuel into your body, you are starving your brain. It's elementary cause and effect. What I see now is that, in so many cases, mental health problems are the result of a bad diet.

Many people put bad fuel into their bodies and expect to feel good. It doesn't work that way. When you give your body bad food, it can't simply convert the bad into good. That's not how the digestive process works. That doesn't happen with any other organism or mechanism in the entire universe. Why would you expect it to happen in your body? You need the right kind and amount of fuel to get your body, and your mind, to peak performance.

You also need to start moving. Ironically, if you're in a bad mental place, you probably don't want to exercise. It might be the last thing you want to do. I get that. After all, I spent an entire summer sitting in a chair watching *The Office* twelve hours a day. I didn't have the desire or interest to get up and move around. If you want to feel better, however, you have to do it. Exercise is vitally important to your mental state, and active people can attest to the fact that, when they feel overwhelmed or anxious, exercise really does improve their mood.

Maybe you're sitting there on the couch right now, and your heart is pounding, your thoughts are racing, and the last thing you want is to go run on a treadmill. I understand how you feel. I really do.

"My heart is already racing, my mind is going a million miles an hour, and you're telling me I need to raise my heart rate even more?"

Yes, that's exactly what I'm saying. And you know what will help you be able to exercise? The right diet. Once you get the right diet in place, you'll have the right fuel to exercise regularly, and once you do that, you're ready for therapy. That's the right order. Diet, exercise, therapy. Put the pieces in place, and you'll start to feel better.

HANGRY

Traditionally, people are told that if they deal with their depression and anxiety through therapy, they'll start to feel better. What I'm saying is that, if you get yourself to feel better physically and get your body to a peak state, then you will get more out of therapy. If you think about it, it's cruel to put someone through therapy while their body continues to malfunction and misfire.

If you put someone through a program to get them feeling good physically, you can then put them into therapy, and therapy will be much more effective. Often, when people feel better physically, they realize that their mental or emotional problems are not as bad as they thought.

If you've ever been "hangry" (hungry + angry), you know what I mean. You get in a bad mood and things get blown out of proportion, but when you finally eat, you realize, "Oh, okay, things are not that bad. I just needed some food." This is the same concept on a broader scale. Make the body feel better, and you'll make the mind feel better. Most people are trying to heal their mental problems first by conventional means, and they don't realize that the most important element in healing the mind is fixing the body.

Wouldn't you like to know what you're doing wrong? Wouldn't you like to know what your doctors have been doing wrong? Brain health leads the way. Let's take a closer look.

Chapter Four

CHASING DOWN HEALTH

———

At one point, I told my girlfriend, "I feel like I'm chasing my health, and no matter what I do, I just can't catch it." The whole experience was incredibly frustrating. It was like being a greyhound at a race track. The gate was down, and the mechanical rabbit was zipping away from me. I was running as fast and as hard as I could, but I just couldn't get any closer. Lap after lap, I ran in fruitless pursuit.

Does that experience sound familiar to you?

MAKING THE CONNECTION

Thanks to my new therapist, I began to see the physical components of my mental health. That alone made a big difference. At the same time, I did have some emotional baggage that I needed to flush out. As I mentioned in the first chapter, I had lingering trauma that had affected me, and therapy provided the perfect space to talk through all those feelings. The therapist helped me to see how events had affected me and influenced my views of myself.

Knowing about the physical connection, however, enabled me to examine my life in a whole new way. I'd had all these strange symptoms plaguing me for so long—the need to eat as soon as I woke up, the need to keep eating every hour or so—and never understood why. After the therapist suggested I was hypoglycemic, I was able to begin monitoring my blood sugar with the glucose meter and eat more frequently.

When I made those simple changes, I started having fewer crashes. It helped, but overall, I still didn't feel good. The anxiety remained, the depression remained, and my brain was foggy all the time. Even with a helpful therapist, I still felt like I was chasing my health.

In my frustration, I remember thinking, "I'm tracking my blood sugar, and I'm eating enough food. I'm crashing less often. Why is my brain always so foggy? Why do I still feel lousy?"

I would often go to Barnes & Noble and stand there pulling books off the shelf one after the other. I read anything related to the topic of happiness or how to be happy. I thought that was my problem: that I lacked happiness, and I'd missed a link somewhere. That's what we all want, isn't it? We want to be happy, yet so many of us have no idea how to get there.

One day, during one of my many excursions to Barnes & Noble, I happened upon a book called *Change Your Brain, Change Your Life* by Dr. Daniel Amen. I flipped to the middle of the book, and an image caught my eye. It was a pair of brain scans set side by side. As I read the caption beneath, I discovered that both scans were from people suffering depression with the same exact symptoms, but the image on the left showed a brain with a low activity level, and the one on the right showed one with a high activity level.

The caption read, "Same exact symptoms, radically different treatments."

This was the moment all the pieces came together for me. Suddenly, everything made sense.

Our thoughts and feelings are not abstract things but a physical reality that can be viewed on a brain scan. When something is wrong with us, when we're having mental health problems, there are brain-structure and activity malfunctions that can be seen, measured, and changed.

It seems like an elementary connection, perhaps, but it's one that many people either fail to make or whose implications they fail to consider. For me, it was the final piece of the puzzle that put me on the path that I'm on today.

I devoured the whole book, and it only confirmed what I'd learned from my therapist. What I was doing to my physical body was contributing to my mental health in a tangible, visible way.

Now I began to realize that mental health problems are not unsolvable, nor are they some mystical phenomenon that can't be understood. We don't have to guess at the solutions. We can see and discover what is happening to the body that is making us feel a certain way mentally and emotionally. When I finally realized that, there was a huge shift in my thinking. Suddenly, there was real hope.

The day I bought the book and read through it, I made the decision to go all in. If there were lifestyle changes I could make to stop this madness, I was ready to make them, whatever that required. Dr. Amen was recommending dietary changes to his patients, encouraging them to start exercising, and getting them started on supplements, and all those things were working. People were getting better.

Dr. Amen wasn't simply dumping strong medication into people, and he wasn't just guessing. He identified physical causes of mental problems, and he worked to change them. I knew if I was going to see the same kind of improvements in my own life, I was going to have to make a 180-degree flip. Everything had to change.

I spent time researching. I dug up everything I could find on subjects like diet, exercise, supplements, meditation, and sleep habits, and I began to make changes. Do you know what I discovered? Improvement came quickly. You might be shocked to hear it, but in just two short weeks, I felt like a completely healed person. After changing my diet, adding exercise and supplements, and improving my sleep habits, I experienced a miraculous recovery. It was truly astounding.

Let's take a look at the things I changed.

DIET

Most people don't realize how profoundly healing food can

be. Conversely, they also don't realize how much damage it can do. I'll give you an example. My girlfriend used to have really bad headaches. All through high school, she complained about migraines that were so bad, she wept from the pain. They followed her into college.

One day, out of the blue, she told me, "Oh, I love bread so much! In high school, I used to come home in the afternoon and grab an entire loaf of bread from the kitchen and devour the whole thing."

I remember thinking, *Okay, that can't be good for you.* I began to observe her symptoms, and I realized that every time she ate bread, she would have migraines the next day.

Finally, I said, "Why don't you stop eating bread for a week and see what happens? See if anything changes?"

She took my suggestion, and the results were immediate. She stopped having the headaches completely. After years of suffering, she got rid of her migraines simply by cutting bread out of her diet.

Have you considered the possibility that the foods you eat are affecting your brain health? Examine what you're putting into your body. Could the wrong foods be causing your

mystery symptoms? Could they be the cause of y
iety and depression, your lack of energy, your hea

Did you know 85 percent of the serotonin in your brain,
which is the specific hormone that makes you feel happy,
is produced in the gut? If your gut is out of whack, you
don't have the proper level of good bacteria, and you
won't get a full dose of serotonin. You'll run short of the
happy hormone. There's a direct link between your diet
and your happiness.[1]

Through much research, study, and experience, I've
adopted what I like to call the "Peak Brain Diet." You've
heard of paleo, and maybe you've heard of the primal
diet, but this diet adds some important things that your
body and your brain really need.

So, what is the Peak Brain Diet? It consists of meat, fruit,
vegetables, nuts, and seeds. That's it. That's the diet I've
adopted, and that's what I eat every day. I've never cheated
on the diet, and, as a result, I've been consistently healthier and happier ever since. It's not hard to stick with it,
thanks to the dramatic results.

Some people hear this, and they balk: "Gosh, you mean

---

1 See Chris Kresser, "Heal Your Gut, Heal Your Brain," ChrisKresser.com, April 28, 2015, https://
chriskresser.com/heal-your-gut-heal-your-brain.

you have to change your whole diet to feel better? I'm not sure I want to do that."

What I tell people is this: "Are you really not that committed to healing your body? Is it not worth the adjustment, if it will make you feel healthy, whole, and completely normal again?"

When I was suffering, I would have eaten raisins for every single meal for the rest of my life if it would have made me feel better. I know I'm not alone in this. There are people out there, and maybe you're one of them, who are ready to do whatever it takes to finally feel good. The right diet is the most important step.

The good news is, on the Peak Brain Diet, I eat fantastic, delicious food. I'm not sitting in a corner like a caveman, gnawing on a root, or staring at a plate with a single stalk of celery on it. I'm enjoying my meals. All I've done is taken out the things that harm my body and added in the things it needs.

SUPPLEMENTS

Zoloft was wreaking havoc on my gut. I spoke about its terrible side effects earlier. It gave me constant diarrhea, had me waking up at three in the morning drenched in sweat, and made me feel generally awful all the time. I really wanted to get off the medication, but I didn't do so immediately.

Stopping a medication suddenly is rarely a good idea. I knew I had to perfect my new lifestyle, adopt the necessary changes, and get to a point where they were a stable part of my life before I got rid of Zoloft. As part of that new lifestyle, I began taking certain supplements to give my body what it really wanted.

What supplements do you need in order to get better? What are you missing? Let's get into it.

VITAMINS C AND D

As you probably already know, the US government puts out a list of average daily recommended amounts of various vitamins and minerals. You see these listed as percentages on ingredient labels. The problem is that the list contains the minimum dosage of what you should be consuming each day. In other words, the government isn't recommending the dose that will lead to optimal health. Instead, what they are telling you is, essentially, "Here's the minimum amount of vitamin C you need each day in order to avoid developing scurvy."

The truth is, for good health, you need to be taking in a huge amount of vitamin C. The same goes for vitamin D. Research indicates that if everyone took two thousand units of vitamin D every day, the cancer rate would decrease by 30 percent. Adding vitamin C and D supplements to your diet is one of the easiest ways to make a big improvement in your health.

OMEGA-3

The brain needs healthy fats. For this reason, you should be consuming plenty of omega-3 fatty acids. A great source of these is fish-oil capsules. Omega-3 provides the brain with the healthy fats it needs to function properly and also acts as an anti-inflammatory. More importantly, it can help people with depression. In one study, one group of patients with depression was put on Prozac, a highly popular antidepressant drug, while another group of depressed patients was given omega-3 fish oils. Surprisingly, the group taking omega-3 experienced much greater improvement in their depression symptoms.[2]

---

2   See S. Jazayeri et al., "Comparison of Therapeutic Effects of Omega-3 Fatty Acid
     Eicosapentaenoic Acid and Fluoxetine, Separately and in Combination, in Major
     Depressive Disorder," *Australian and New Zealand Journal of Psychiatry* 42, no. 3 (March
     2008): 192–98, https://www.ncbi.nlm.nih.gov/pubmed/18247193. See also Y. Osher and
     R. H. Belmaker, "Omega-3 Fatty Acids in Depression: A Review of Three Studies," *CNS
     Neuroscience & Therapeutics* 15, no. 2 (Summer 2009): 128–33, https://www.ncbi.nlm.nih.gov/
     pubmed/19499625.

Prozac has many severe side effects and is not even as effective as a natural supplement. It's so much easier and safer to walk down to the local drugstore and pick up some omega-3 capsules than to get on Prozac and deal with all the negative side effects.

EXERCISE

Exercise is important for your mental health, but I'm not suggesting you have to start pumping iron or running triathlons. In fact, the exercise routine you create for yourself doesn't have to be grueling. All I recommend to people is that they take regular walks. If you'll just start walking three to five times a week for thirty minutes to an hour, it will make a big difference.

Think back to the hunter-gatherer days of our ancestors. People regularly walked for long periods of time. They didn't have a choice. They walked to one place to hunt, then to another place to sleep. They might do a little running along the way, perhaps when evading attackers, but they weren't going on grueling ten-mile runs every day. Mostly, they just walked, and that's what our bodies are designed to do. Later on, we'll discuss the effect of exercise on your mood and mental health in greater depth.

MEDITATION

What do I mean when I say meditation? Most people hear that word and think about someone sitting cross-legged with their hands in the air, listening to a musician thumping on a drum. Although you are certainly free to do that if you wish, meditation happens any time you intentionally go off by yourself. It's peaceful time, alone time.

For example, you might listen to music and take a walk. That's a great way to meditate. Personally, I like to listen to podcasts while I walk, so that's my version of meditation. I'll walk for an hour and listen to a podcast. It gets me away from daily stresses, gives me time to quietly reflect on things, and provides exercise. I feel great afterward. It also gives me time for self-improvement, which is the reason for the podcasts.

SLEEP

The importance of healthy sleeping habits cannot be overstated. You absolutely need seven to nine hours of sleep a night. If you get less than that, you are robbing your brain of the essential rest it needs to stay healthy. If your lifestyle is preventing you from getting seven to nine hours of sleep a night, then make whatever changes you have to make to get there. There is no substitute for sleep, which means there is no way for your brain to make up for a lack of it.

THERAPY

As I've mentioned, there might be some trauma in your life that is contributing to your anxiety and depression. For this reason, I recommend therapy alongside other lifestyle changes. Don't be afraid to dive deep and discover what's affecting you. Because of the embarrassment associated with therapy, some people hold back during sessions. They don't open up completely.

I had that problem at first, but I wanted to get better so badly that eventually I decided I wasn't going to hold anything back. I knew that if I didn't want to relapse because of emotional trauma from my past, I had to put it all out there. When I opened up completely, I was able to work through everything, deal with it, and move on. A good therapist will always make it feel safe for you to talk openly and honestly.

A HIGHER POWER

Another thing I'll add, because it's been instrumental in my life, is the importance of faith in the process of healing. I don't believe that God caused these bad things to happen to me, but He definitely held the door open and let me walk through it, because He had a lot to teach me. I also believe that God was intimately involved in my healing. Personally, I receive a huge sense of relief knowing that God is protecting me, and that He doesn't want me to suffer. Even though it's your choice whether or not to have faith in God, it is my conviction that it is the single most important part of a person's life.

WHERE I AM NOW

These were the major changes I made to my lifestyle, and I'll be honest, the first week was difficult. The changes were a shock to my body, and I had some hard habits to break. We forget how ingrained some of our habits are until we attempt to get rid of them. However, after that first week, I started to feel the change, and then it happened. Suddenly, one morning, I woke up, and it was like someone had flipped on the lights in a dark house. I felt fantastic.

How am I doing now? It is no exaggeration to say that with these lifestyle changes, I feel completely healed. I have never felt better in my entire life than I do right now. I had no idea that it was possible to feel this good. Thanks to research and experience, I am confident in the knowledge that I have acquired about my health. So, when I say I miraculously healed myself, I mean it. And I know others who have done so as well.

I feel incredibly healthy and mentally stronger than ever. I no longer suffer from anxiety or depression, and my thoughts are crystal clear. Yes, I deal with the normal stresses of life, but knowing that my feelings are connected to real events is strangely exciting. For example, I might get butterflies in my stomach when I'm about to speak in front of a large crowd. That's a natural feeling, and I love it. The unexplained, free-floating symptoms are gone.

THE RIGHT TOOLS

My story, when you boil it down to its essence, is a simple one. I was suffering from anxiety, depression, OCD, and intrusive thoughts. Some of this was triggered by sexual abuse, some of it came from my dad's battle with cancer, but a lot if it came out of nowhere. No matter what I did, my situation got worse and worse. I didn't know where to turn, and I couldn't find the right help.

Eventually, life became hell. I mean that literally—I experienced what hell must be like. From the time I opened my eyes in the morning until the wee hours of the night, I suffered, and it was terrible. And then, through research and self-experimentation, I found the right tools to help myself. I healed my body, I healed my brain, and I turned everything around.

I want everyone to experience this same miraculous recovery. You see, it's not difficult to get there. All you have to do is give your body the building blocks it needs and wants to function properly. When you do that, your body will begin to put itself back together.

There's so much good, healthy food out there, but if you continue giving your body junk, it's going to continue to feel bad. Change your diet, start taking supplements, treat your body well, and you'll feel the results quicker than you might expect.

I want you to get your hands on the right tools, so you can experience the same healing that I did, because I know there is a far better, happier life waiting for you.

Chapter Five

IT'S BRAIN HEALTH, NOT MENTAL HEALTH

———

What's the difference between mental health and brain health? It's largely a matter of perception. In other words, the difference lies in the way we think of the terms; and only one of them points to the connection between mental and physical health.

When we talk about "mental health," it's easy to think of something abstract, or disconnected from the body, and that contributes to the idea that it's a separate issue.

The term "brain health," on the other hand, drives home the fact that our mental health problems are malfunctions of an actual physical organ in the body. Changes in mood, struggles with negative emotions, and bad thoughts are all physical realities and need to be understood and approached as such.

When someone stays up late, eats a lot of pizza, and then goes right to bed, they probably expect to wake up the next morning with digestive problems. When someone skips meals, they expect to feel hungry later. But how many people eat junk food and expect to feel depressed as a result? How many people skip a meal and expect to feel anxiety a few hours later? This is where the connection usually breaks down.

Brain health problems are a reflection of physical ailments. If you're not treating your body right, your brain will become deficient, and that will directly affect your emotional state.

When I was going through my crisis, I had a bad habit of not eating throughout the day, because I felt sick and anxious. When I went to buy a suit with my father, and we stopped to get something to eat beforehand, I sat there staring at a tray of food. None of it looked good to me, so I scarcely ate anything.

That happened to me frequently in those days. I had a diminished appetite. At most meals, I'd force down a few bites or peck at my food, but I was practically fasting all day long. Then I'd go to bed at night and try to sleep, and I'd wake up feeling even sicker and more miserable.

There was a compounding effect. The day I went to the store with my parents and had a panic attack, I was basically feeling the negative effects of not eating. But I didn't know that at the time. I thought something was seriously wrong with me. Instead, my body was just desperate for good, healthy fuel.

BRAIN SCANS

Since the brain is a physical part of the body, a brain scan gives a clear picture of what's going on. I recommend getting a SPECT scan to find out if your brain is healthy. SPECT stands for Single Photon Emission Computed Tomography. Using a small dose of a radioactive isotope as a tracer, it measures blood flow and brain activity. Unlike a CAT scan, which primarily shows the brain's structure, a SPECT scan tells you how the brain is functioning.

The scans aren't cheap, but they're a great way to quickly identify problems in brain activity. If you really want to figure out whether or not there's a physical problem in your brain, then it's worth the cost.

One reason this is important is because patients with different types of problems can have the same symptoms. As I learned from that image in Dr. Amen's book, some people experience depression as a result of low brain activity. Others might feel the same as a result of high brain activity. That's true of anxiety as well. It's important to differentiate because if you give the same medication to both people, it's going to be really bad for at least one of them. Treatment needs to be tailored to the health of your particular brain.

Dr. Amen is one of the few psychiatrists who examines brain function with SPECT scans to treat patients with mental health problems. These scans reveal changes and problem areas, and ultimately they confirm whether or not the problem can be treated by diet alone, if there's a need for surgery, or, in rare cases, if there's a need for medication. If you're struggling with mental health problems, and you've never had a SPECT scan, I highly recommend it. The results can be illuminating.

LOOKING BEYOND MEDS

The danger of psychiatric medication is greater than the awful side effects. In fact, many of these medications can do actual damage to the brain, particularly when taken at a young age. It deeply saddens me when I hear about elementary- and middle-school children being put on medication to treat conditions like ADD and ADHD. I know people who were put on antianxiety medication as early as eighth grade.

This is so bad for brain health. When you're in elementary or middle school, your brain hasn't finished developing, so strong medication has the potential to negatively affect that development.

Doctors are treating children by covering up symptoms such as anxiety, depression, and hyperactivity and, in the process, are altering brain development and creating lifelong consequences. This is so unnecessary when there are other, healthier ways to treat people. After all, the symptoms are basically expressions of bigger problems.

If there's any risk of harming a child's brain development, doesn't it make sense to try everything else first? If a child is introduced to a healthier diet, and this doesn't alleviate their emotional problems immediately, at least no permanent damage has been done. Sadly, many people turn to medication first, before considering other options.

Wouldn't you much rather get better by changing your diet instead of getting on psychiatric drugs that are going to wreak havoc on your body and flood you with all these side effects? If you're struggling with medication right now, isn't it worth it to find out how much better you could feel with a healthier diet?

I know a lot of people taking psychiatric drugs of one kind or another, and I can't think of a single one of them who would say, "Yes, on this drug, I feel great, and I'm all better!" Not a single one. Instead, they are suffering the side effects, and on top of that, they're all still anxious and depressed. Why do they keep taking the medication? Because doctors tell them to. They've been led to believe it's their only hope.

CUSTOMIZE YOUR PLAN

I talked about the Peak Brain Diet in general terms: meat, fruit, vegetables, nuts, and seeds. But you can tailor the diet to your specific symptoms. You can also tailor the supplements you're taking to your specific needs. Whatever you do, I highly recommend that you take the same supplements at the same time every day. Once your body starts getting a big dose of the nutrients it needs, it will begin to expect them.

When it comes to exercise, you can come up with a plan that works best for you. Maybe you enjoy taking a walk early in the morning, or maybe you prefer some light

exercise in the afternoon. It's up to you, so long as you g
your body moving on a regular basis. Make it work wit
your schedule and your life. Also get plenty of sleep at the
end of the day. The same goes for therapy. I recommend
once a week, but make it work for you. Do it as often as you
find necessary to deal with whatever you're going through.

COLLEGE STUDENTS ARE SUFFERING

Ultimately, you've got to stop ingesting so much added
sugar, so many artificial ingredients, and wheat and grains.
It's as simple as that. You can no longer deprive your body
of the nutrients it needs, the sleep it needs, or the vitamins
and minerals it needs. You've got to stop holding on to
emotional distress. Until you make these changes, you
will continue to have mental problems.

Sadly, I've just described the vast majority of college students on American university campuses today. I meet so
many college students who don't feel mentally or emotionally healthy. When I tell them about the things in their
diet and lifestyle that are harming them, often they'll
initially reply by saying, "Well, that's not really an issue
for me. My diet and lifestyle are okay."

Then I get them to look at their lives a little more closely,
and you know what I almost always find? They are indeed

staying up way too late most days. They're eating junk food filled with chemicals that shouldn't be there. They're taking in way too much processed sugar. They don't take vitamins or supplements of any kind, so their bodies lack essential nutrients. They aren't active. They might walk to class, but that's not enough exercise. Most of the time they are sitting or lying around.

These are the same poor souls who say, "Gosh, I feel this crippling anxiety all the time, so I have to get on some medication." Can't you see that's not the answer? Clearly, there is a problem with your body.

Haven't you ever noticed that the big health geeks, the guys and girls who are hanging out at the gym seven days a week, who only eat chicken and vegetables every meal and take handfuls of supplements every day, are never the ones who say, "Oh, I feel so tired all the time. I feel like crap. I need medication."

Typically, they're the ones who come bounding into the room full of energy. It's because they are eating healthy food and treating their bodies right. Look at the people around you who are truly happy, healthy, and full of energy and zest for life. Examine the way they're living, what they eat, and how often they exercise. In almost every case, you will see the difference reflected in their lifestyles.

EXAMINE YOUR LIFE

Haven't you suffered long enough? Isn't it time to finally make the changes that are going to bring you greater happiness? Let this be the moment when you start to develop a new routine that's going to train your body and your brain. If you really want to fix your mental health problems and stop feeling like crap, then start making those lifestyle changes today. These changes aren't going to take anything away from your life, but instead will add greatly to it.

Examine your diet closely. What are you eating? If your diet is full of processed sugar, wheat and grains, and other things that are making you sick, get rid of them. Take those things out of your life. You might think, "I'll have to get rid of so many things I enjoy!" But think of the value you're adding to your life, because now you'll be healthy. Isn't it worth missing your favorite sugary snacks and fried foods if it means you'll be able to give your loved ones 100 percent of your attention, and you'll be able to function properly?

It's worth it. Trust me. Examine your life, and start making those changes today.

Chapter Six

GIVE YOUR BODY WHAT IT WANTS

———

THE RIGHT FOOD, SUPPLEMENTS, EXERCISE, AND SLEEP

THE KEYS TO ENSURING BRAIN HEALTH

Glucose is your brain's fuel source. Your brain needs enough to function properly. A healthy range is between 75 and 95 mg/dl, so anything below that is problematic. Around 50 mg/dl, you can actually pass out and suffer brain damage.

If it's possible to suffer brain damage from low blood sugar, then clearly this is something that everyone needs to pay attention to. If you're not in the safe range, you're going to begin to experience mental and emotional changes, along with physical problems.

Blood sugar has been called the great imposter because, when it gets low, the body senses an emergency and reacts as if it were under attack. Adrenaline and cortisol are pumped into the bloodstream, and you start feeling anxious. Physical symptoms include sweating, rapid heartbeat, heightened senses, tingling, and a prolonged sinking sensation.

All those symptoms are necessary in the event of an actual physical threat, but in the case of low blood sugar, they don't actually help. There is no immediate cause in your environment for the panic you feel. You might just be driving somewhere, going about your day, and suddenly that classic anxious feeling comes right back to you. Your body is screaming at you, "Get me out of here! Run! Hurry!"

When people treat anxiety, they rarely consider the much simpler possibility that they just need to eat the right food more frequently. It's such an easy solution, but so many turn to antianxiety medication instead. Unfortunately, one of the side effects of antianxiety medication is hunger suppression, so now you don't feel like doing the one thing you really need to do.

The body is crying out for more blood sugar to feed the brain, but medication is masking that feeling and diminishing appetite. The brain continues to be starved for fuel, while you wonder why your medication isn't helping as much as it should. It's a dreadful, endless cycle of misery.

BLOOD SUGAR AND DEPRESSION

What is blood sugar's connection to depression? When your brain is low on fuel, activity slows down. The brain is forced to choose which parts are most vital and which can afford to be starved. The prefrontal cortex, which handles decision-making, is usually neglected first. That means you begin struggling to make decisions. Your thoughts become foggy, and you slow down. Over time, you sink into depression.

You've probably experienced a mild form of this when you're hungry. When you need something to eat, you might have trouble concentrating. What you probably don't realize is that this is happening because your brain is being forced to prioritize.

Even people who aren't hypoglycemic benefit from feeding their brains throughout the day. I'm not talking about overeating. That's important to clarify. Don't take in more calories than you need. I'm talking about eating at a consistent rate. This includes snacking between meals.

A handful of nuts is perfect because they're high in healthy fat. This helps keep your blood sugar up, and that, in turn, helps you maintain optimal mental health all day long. It also keeps your hormone levels up and your adrenal glands and cortisol in check. It's a good idea all around.

FOOD	
Type	Variations
Meats	Beef, chicken, pork, etc.
Fruits	Apples, strawberries, bananas, etc.
Vegetables	Broccoli, green beans, squash, etc.
Nuts & Seeds	Almonds, brazil nuts, cashews, etc.

THE PEAK BRAIN DIET

Let's take a closer look at the Peak Brain Diet. The idea behind it is simple: avoid the foods that affect the brain negatively, and increase the intake of the foods it needs. It's a matter of figuring out what those are.

Added sugar is the worst. Scientists have done PET brain scans on people who are addicted to cocaine and compared them to the PET brain scans of people who eat a lot of added sugar. The results look exactly the same. It's a startling result. Whether it's an addiction to smoking, alcohol, cocaine, or sugar, the physical effect on the brain is exactly the same.[1]

Often, when someone with anxiety or depression is having a really bad episode, you can track what they eat and drink to find an immediate, contributing cause in their diet. For example, they might have ingested a huge Frappuccino at Starbucks, or a bunch of candy, or, as in the case of my girlfriend, a whole loaf of bread. You might not realize just how much sugar there is in a nondessert item like a loaf of bread.

What happens is that all the added sugar gets digested faster than it should, because these food items lack fiber and include added rather than naturally occurring sugars. As a result, the blood-sugar level spikes and then crashes dramatically. This puts the body and brain on a terrible rollercoaster ride, sending the body into a state of emergency. The body feels like it's under attack and sends out adrenaline.

There are so many people going through this cycle all the time, day after day, without understanding why. They are constantly sick and miserable, and maybe they've even

---

1   See Tom McKay, "What Happens to Your Brain on Sugar, Explained by Science," Mic.com, April 21, 2014, https://mic.com/articles/88015/what-happens-to-your-brain-on-sugar-explained-by-science.

concluded that this is simply how the body is supposed to feel. It has, after all, become their version of normal.

Not many people would try to argue the case that added sugar is good for the body, but I don't think enough people realize just how bad it really is. Let me illustrate the danger with another example.

PET scans are used on cancer patients to detect tumors and cancer spots. Doctors give a patient a sugary drink that has radioactive isotopes in it, because about an hour after drinking it, every spot of cancer will light up on the scan. Why does every spot of cancer light up? Because sugar rushes to all the cancer spots. That's because sugar is cancer's main food source, and most people are gorging themselves on it every day.

WHEAT AND GRAINS

Some people are surprised to learn that wheat and grains are not good for your health. They inflame the body, especially the gut, which ends up inflaming the brain. A lot of people find this hard to believe. How can wheat be bad for you? When I've shared this with people, some have even responded with, "Wait a minute. Jesus ate bread and grain, so it's been a staple food for a long, long time."

The grain Jesus was eating two thousand years ago and the grain we're eating today have very little in common. Wheat back then was much smaller and easier to digest. Now, thanks to human tampering, our wheat is huge and has been modified. It's almost a completely different food.

When wheat inflames the body, you can see the consequences physically. People who eat a lot of wheat tend to be overweight, and their necks and cheeks are often red. They seem stuffed and uncomfortable all the time. It's because their bodies are practically on fire from all the wheat and grains they're eating.

This is the body's way of saying, "Please, stop feeding the fire that's inside of me with all this sugar, grain, and wheat products!"

ARTIFICIAL INGREDIENTS

Go to any local grocery store, and pick a food item off the shelves at random. Flip over the box and read the ingredients. You'll see things on that list that you've never heard of, things almost nobody has ever heard of.

On an almost daily basis, people say to me, "I feel like there's so much more cancer in the world these days. Every time I turn around, somebody is getting cancer. What is causing this? What has gone so wrong with us?"

You know what I tell them? "It's because we're eating poison. Of course we're getting cancer. We are literally filling our bodies with poisonous, hazardous materials every single day, meal after meal after meal."

Here's one example. Splenda, the artificial, no-calorie sweetener, was discovered by accident during the making of a pesticide. They mixed the wrong chemicals, and suddenly Splenda was born. And people are dumping it into their coffee and tea every day.

If your artificial sweetener was created as an accidental by-product in the manufacture of pesticide, then maybe, just maybe, you shouldn't be putting it into your body. Artificial sweeteners like this overload the body and jack up hormone levels.

All these strange, artificial ingredients being put into our foods are terrible for your body. Your body is being forced to digest these unnatural ingredients and figure out what to do with them daily. Most people don't know why they're in the food to begin with, but, unfortunately, not enough of them care to find out.

The purpose of most of the strange chemicals in processed food is to extend shelf life. In the food-production business, extending shelf life contributes to profitability, so companies will do whatever they can to make their food products last longer. They clearly don't care what effect these chemicals have on the body, and the people who buy and consume the products don't seem to mind. If customers wind up feeling anxious or depressed, they just assume they must be sad about something.

In reality, these people are feeling the aftereffects of ingesting poison. Some of what is being put into processed food we are simply not designed to eat. Our bodies don't want these poisons.

The people you see walking around in peak physical health, full of energy and taking on life's challenges with gusto, aren't filling their bodies with this processed garbage, and you can see the difference. The people who are consuming delivery pizza late at night in their dorm rooms, then waking up and having Pop Tarts and a soda before heading off to class, are not the people who are going out with enthusiasm and conquering the world. They never really feel good and slog through each day just trying to survive.

Now that you have an idea of a few of the things you shouldn't be eating, let's look a little closer at some of the positive foods you need. First of all, you need to be eating foods that are high in healthy fat. You might remember the food pyramid that the US government first put out in 1992. Posters of it used to hang in school cafeterias. The purpose of the food pyramid was to show people how much of each food group they should be consuming.

Do you recall the largest section of the food pyramid? Grains. The government was telling people, "You really need to eat a lot of wheat and grains and gluten products, because that's what we're supposed to do to stay healthy." At the same time, they were telling people to cut out fats. "Fat is terrible. Fat makes you fat. Get rid of it."

So what happened? Food labs across the country started working furiously to create low-fat food products. Many popular food brands put out low-fat or no-fat alternatives.

In reality, as we know now, things are the other way around. Wheat and grains are the last things you should be gorging on. Fats are what you should be eating, the healthy kinds of fat. They are great for your brain health. Where do you get these healthy fats? From avocados, from nuts and seeds, from chicken. All these foods have high fat content.

Your brain is basically made up of fat, so it needs healthy fat to function properly. And for years, companies were cutting out fat and leaving in wheat and grains. No wonder recent generations have suffered from so many mental and emotional problems, physical ailments, and obesity.

Healthy fats also help your body hold on to blood sugar longer. If, for example, you eat an avocado in the morning with some nuts and seeds, and maybe a piece of fish or chicken for lunch, you will keep your blood sugar much more stable from morning to night than if your diet is mostly grains. You will feel the difference: no more spiking and no more crashing.

Another response I get from people when they hear about this diet is, "Well, if I'm cutting out all the wheat and grains from my diet, if I'm eliminating bread and pasta, how am I going to get my carbs?"

Vegetables are an excellent source of carbohydrates. They are healthy carbs that are good for your body. I recommend eating some vegetables in the morning. I know that might sound strange. Who eats veggies for breakfast?

However, vegetables in the morning provide carbs that will sustain you.

My recommendation for the perfect breakfast? Chicken or eggs with a side of vegetables. Specifically, I suggest green beans or broccoli with half an avocado. That meal provides protein from the chicken or eggs, carbs from the vegetables, and then healthy fat from the avocado to hold it all in.

FRUIT

What about fruit? The good news is you don't have to cut fruit completely out of your diet. But eat it in moderation. Something to keep in mind is that the sugar in fruit is not glucose but fructose. That's still sugar, but at least it's a naturally occurring fruit sugar. The beauty of fruit is that the sugary juice is surrounded by lots of fiber, which helps your body digest it at a consistent rate.

Avoid fruit juice! If you're going to drink a glass of orange juice, you might as well just drink a Coke. Either way, the sugar is going to be digested immediately, and your blood sugar will spike. The problem is that fruit juice doesn't have fibrous covering around it, and your body needs that fiber to digest the sugar slowly and properly.

I also recommend that you avoid smoothies. They have

the same problems that juice does. A lot of the fiber is pulverized in the production of smoothies, so they're not all that different from drinking a soda. If you don't believe me, look at the sugar content of your favorite smoothie.

IS ORGANIC IMPORTANT?

Should you buy organic foods or foods labeled organic? It's not bad to do so, but it doesn't necessarily matter. When a food is labeled organic, that doesn't mean as much as you might think. For example, with vegetables, all it usually means is that they weren't sprayed with pesticide. As long as you wash your fruit and vegetables, you are fine.

The same goes for chicken. Whether or not it's organic, as far as your health goes, you're getting the same product. If you're into organic food, and you want to go that route, it's perfectly fine. It's a great choice to make, but it's not necessary.

THE COST

"Eating healthy is too expensive!"

That's a complaint I hear all the time.

You could go to the grocery store right now and get a

seven-pack of chicken breasts for about thirteen dollars, depending on the cost of living in your area. Then you could head over to the produce section and get a pound of broccoli for roughly a dollar. That's about fifteen dollars total, including sales tax, and it will last for an entire week of lunches.

Fifteen dollars for a week of lunches is not a bad deal. Then, if you wanted, you could add a carton of eggs. The point is, eating healthy is really not that expensive. You can eat good food every day of the week for a reasonable price, as long as you shop wisely. Don't make cost your excuse.

SUPPLEMENTS	
Type	Amount
Vitamin D	2,000IU
Vitamin C	2,000- 10,000mg
Omega 3	2,000-4,000mg higher EPA
Ginko	120mg
Probiotic	20-50 billion cultures
Blood Sugar	
CoQ10	100-150mg
Cinnamon + Chromium	2,000mg
Anxiety	
GABA	100-250mg
Depression	
St. John's Wort	200-500mg
5-HTP	100mg

This handy chart will help you understand which supplements you need and how much you should be taking. Vitamin C, in particular, is best in high doses, not just 750 mg. I recommend 2–10 grams. That's 2,000–10,000 mg. That amount of vitamin C washes the toxins out of your body.

Vitamin D, despite its name, isn't really a vitamin. It's a hormone, and it's essential for good health. If you have the wrong level of vitamin D in your diet, you're going to have problems. It's possible to have too little or too much vitamin D. Either way, you will experience negative side effects, so finding the right dosage is important.

I once knew a guy who was going through cancer treatment, and the doctor was giving him high doses of vitamin D. He started experiencing terrible depressed episodes. He couldn't snap out of it. When they did a test on him, they discovered that he was toxic with vitamin D. They brought the dosage down, and he completely stabilized. Make sure you're getting the right amount. In general, 2,000 mg a day is perfect.

Though vitamins C and D are important, they are not enough. You should also be taking omega-3 fish oils. Take a look at the chart for a clear understanding of how much

e. If omega-3 supplements aren't already part of diet, you should add them right away.

Another supplement I recommend is gingko. It's an herbal supplement that increases blood flow in the brain. Benefits include improved memory. I take it every day. In general, I also recommend taking a good multivitamin, but I advise people to avoid tablets because they include various chemicals that act as binders to hold them together. In fact, I recommend vegetable-gel capsules for everything you take.

If you're having blood-sugar problems, Coenzyme Q10 (CoQ10) can help. It's one of the pricier supplements, costing around forty dollars a month. However, it can help you get your blood sugar under control. It's not necessary to take it indefinitely. As a short-term solution, it can help with blood sugar, and afterward, you can simply transition to a good multivitamin.

Two other natural supplements that can help with blood sugar are cinnamon and chromium. You can actually buy these together. Nature's Bounty offers a good cinnamon and chromium supplement. Take it in the morning along with your healthy breakfast. You'll feel great all day long.

If you're having anxiety and depression problems in par-

ticular, then you need a good probiotic. Remember
percent of your serotonin, the happy drug for your br.
is produced in the gut. One of the unfortunate side effects
of the SSRI (selective serotonin reuptake inhibitor) anti-
depression medications people are prescribed is that they
damage your gut. That's the reason why I had so many
digestive and stomach problems when I was taking Zoloft.

When you mess up your gut with medication, then you
decrease your serotonin level, and that makes your mental
health situation worse. If you want a healthy brain, you
need a healthy gut.

I recommend about fifty billion cultures of a good probiotic. Some probiotic formulas need to be refrigerated,
while others don't, but it doesn't matter which way you go.
Just make sure to use vegetable-gel capsules, and make
sure the cultures are live, which work more effectively.

If you're dealing specifically with anxiety, GABA (gamma-
Aminobutyric acid) is a fantastic supplement to include
in your regimen. GABA is a neurotransmitter that helps
calm the brain.

For depression, I recommend 5-HTP or St. John's wort.
Both of these are fantastic for raising serotonin levels in
the brain and act as natural SSRIs.

EVERYONE IS DIFFERENT

I recognize that everyone is different, and the way you transition into this new diet might differ from the way I did. I was sick and tired of feeling miserable. I'd had enough, so, in one day, I changed my diet completely and started taking a handful of supplements. The change was dramatic.

Some people might think that's too much to handle all at once. As far as supplements go, you can introduce them into your diet slowly, if you prefer. However, if you want fast results and dramatic changes, I encourage you to go for it. Make the lifestyle changes. Make them all at once, and don't look back!

After all, what's so bad about feeling good all the time? With all that you've suffered, is there really any reason to hold back? The way I look at it, if you're going to do something, you might as well go all the way. You did it with medication. One day, you just started taking it. Why not do the same with these healthy changes that are actually going to bring about healing?

ARE YOU SLEEPING?

There is actually a chemical that's released while you sleep that physically washes the brain. Everything that's happened to you during the day is processed, and brain connections are reset. This prepares you to face a new day. Without enough sleep, this natural process doesn't take place fully. It's why you get foggy-headed when you're sleep-deprived.

Don't forget, our hunter-gatherer ancestors slept from shortly after the sun went down until the sun came up again. Can you imagine sleeping from 7:30 p.m. to 6:00 a.m.? But that's what they did, so it's what our bodies are adapted for. We are designed to get a full cycle of sleep; our brains need it.

Our habits today are much different than our ancestors'. With the invention of the light bulb, we can stay up as late as we want, and because of computers and electronics, most people are up way past sunset, playing games, watching shows, or working on projects. It's yet another aspect of modern life that contributes to bad mental health, because the brain can't function well on too little sleep.

It's like never turning off your car. Can you imagine if you drove your car home at the end of the day, pulled it into the driveway, put it in park, and then left it running all night? Over time, the car would wear out faster and have more problems, even if you kept putting fuel into the tank.

Instead, you take your car home, park it, and turn it off.

Why? Because even though it's a machine, you recognize that it needs to rest. You let your car rest everywhere you take it. You don't leave it running in the parking lot while you shop or go to a restaurant, because you know it would be harder on the engine.

If we understand this about vehicles, why don't we understand it about the brain? The brain needs the proper amount of rest every night, so it can wash itself and recover. Make appropriate lifestyle changes so that you're getting those seven to nine hours. Do what you have to do. Turn off the television, turn off the computer, put away that project, and go to bed. Your brain will thank you for it, and you'll feel better.

A STRICT PROGRAM

I keep myself on a strict program because I don't like the way I feel when I go off of it. The one time I went off the healthy diet, it didn't take long to feel the difference. It was spring break, and my girlfriend, her best friend, and I decided to take a trip to California to visit Disneyland. We flew out on a Sunday, intending to stay through Thursday. I brought all my supplements with me, as I do whenever I travel.

Because we were on vacation and having fun, there were a few mornings when I forgot to take my supplements at the hotel. I was excited, looking forward to the park, and it just slipped my mind. By the time I remembered my supplements, it was already the middle of the day, we were in the park, and the supplements were back in the hotel room. I figured it wasn't a big deal. Surely, I could skip a few days without hurting myself.

I also got lax about my diet. Theme parks don't have the healthiest food, as most people know from experience. It's a magical land of indulgence and fried food, but I did the best I could. They sold mangoes throughout the park, so I ate a lot of mango. Fruit in moderation is fine, as I've said, but mangoes are really high on the glycemic index. On top of that, I couldn't resist enjoying some chocolate and chocolate-covered strawberries from the gift shop. I typically eat dark chocolate because it's healthier for you. These were milk chocolate, but I thought, "Oh, a little bit here and there will be fine."

At restaurants, I made some poor choices. One night in Laguna Beach, I ordered chicken marsala. When it came out, I saw that the chicken breast was breaded. Instead of sending it back, which I normally would have done, I said, "You know what? It's okay. I'm on vacation. It'll be fine this one time." I hadn't eaten bread in months, and I was feeling so much better for it. But here we were on vacation, living it up, so I ate the breaded chicken.

Later that night, I started to feel my health deteriorate. The next day, I woke up, and I was a mess. I'd gotten used to feeling great, to having energy and being in a good mood all the time. Slipping back into that old, unhealthy state was startling. I felt sick and anxious, and the contrast was stark.

In the end, that experience was a positive, because it reminded me just how much food actually impacts my health and attitude. If anything, it was an affirmation of the lifestyle changes I'd made. The deterioration was noticeable after only a few days. I hadn't gone off the diet completely. All I did was cheat a little bit, skip my supplements a few times, and eat a few things I usually avoid, but that's all it took to put me back in a bad place.

You might not even realize that the way you're feeling each day is not the way you're supposed to feel. You lack energy, you feel moody and anxious, you're uncomfortable all the time, and you don't realize that it's not normal. Your body is complaining about your diet and lifestyle.

You can't fully understand the awful effects an unhealthy diet has on your whole being until you've experienced the alternative. When you make the necessary changes, eventually you start to take for granted just how good you feel. The initial shock wears off, and you just enjoy that good feeling every day. It becomes normal, as it should. This is how your body wants to feel. This is how your brain wants to feel. This is what a healthy human existence is supposed to be.

When you go back to the old diet and the good feeling slips away, it drives home just how amazing the difference is. If you haven't experienced it for yourself, you really have no idea how much better things could be or how good you could feel.

If you want to feel better, make the changes you need to make in order to improve your lifestyle, and stick with them. Aren't you curious to discover what it feels like to be a truly healthy, happy human being? You can. The tools are available to you.

Chapter Seven

PHYSICAL THERAPY
FOR YOUR MIND

———

Let's look a little closer at the role therapy plays in this new, healthier lifestyle. I really see therapy as the quarterback of your emotional health, helping to put all the pieces of your life in the right places. When you're struggling on your own, some experiences can get blown out of proportion, other things can get repressed, and still other things can cause confusion. A lot of people go through life feeling mixed up, and it's difficult to step back and take a broader look at life.

In order to deal with what you're going through, you need an opportunity to speak openly and honestly. You need to be able to talk through your issues with a professional.

When you do that, you're able to come to terms with what has happened to you.

But therapy is not just about dealing with past trauma. I recommend going once a week, so you can talk about whatever might be going on in your life at the moment, both good and bad. This keeps things from building up.

IT'S NOT A SUBSTITUTE

To clarify, therapy is very helpful, but it's not enough by itself. It can be tempting to use therapy as a substitute for all the changes I've discussed in this book. It sounds so much easier, doesn't it? Why adjust to a new diet and exercise regimen, and buy a bunch of supplements, if you can just talk to someone and get better?

While an exhaustive amount of therapy over many years might eventually train your brain to compensate for physical vulnerabilities, it's so much easier when you smooth the way by making your body and brain as healthy as possible.

This book is a precursor to therapy. These lifestyle changes make therapy more effective. You first have to get your body and your brain level, so don't charge into therapy until you've adjusted to the new diet, sleep schedule, and exercise routine.

One of the biggest reasons why so many people today aren't making progress in overcoming their mental and emotional problems, despite years of effort, is because they get things backward. "If I fix my depression and anxiety, then I'll feel better physically."

No, it's the other way around. Fix the way you feel physically, and you'll find yourself in a better mental and emotional state. Once I fixed my body, I didn't have debilitating physical symptoms dominating my life, and that allowed me to focus on other things during therapy.

A visit to the therapist is like physical therapy for your brain. When you a break a limb, you first set the bone and get it healing. After that, you might have to go to physical therapy for a while to rejuvenate the limb and rebuild its strength. In every other area of health, when something is broken, you deal with what's broken first, get it to heal, and then you spend time rehabilitating it.

You'll get so much more out of your therapy sessions that way. And when you get more out of each session, therapy winds up being far more cost-effective. That's a great incentive if you're worried about the cost of therapy: get more accomplished in fewer sessions, and save money!

A bad diet, lack of exercise, and lack of sleep heighten your feelings. This is why you feel as if you've been hit with a ton of bricks when some minor frustration occurs. Your feelings are not commensurate with the actual magnitude of the circumstances, because your brain isn't functioning properly. It's why so many people are struck down by routine problems—a bad grade, an argument with a loved one, car problems, a minor injury—and what most of them don't realize is that their diet and lifestyle have made them vulnerable. It sounds crazy, but it's true.

Have you set yourself up for serious emotional problems by being unaware of your body's needs? Without realizing it, I had laid the groundwork for the mental health crisis I experienced that summer. I had no idea that the terrible food I was eating, my lack of exercise, poor sleep, and the residue of past trauma were all festering inside of me, just waiting for some stressful circumstance to make the symptoms manifest. Like most people, I went through life unaware of the ways I was creating the conditions for mental health problems.

All of the things I'm recommending work together to make your life better. Remember, it's a holistic approach—

seeing yourself not as isolated systems, but as a whole person, with every organ connected and working together.

THE FIRST STEP

YOUR NEW DAY!

SUPPLEMENTS	
Type	**Amount**
Vitamin D	2,000IU
Vitamin C	2,000-10,000mg
Omega 3	2,000-4,000mg higher EPA
Ginko	120mg
Probiotic	20-50 billion cultures
Blood Sugar	
CoQ10	100-150mg
Cinnamon + Chromium	2,000mg
Anxiety	
GABA	100-250mg
Depression	
St. Johns Wort	200-500mg
5-HTP	100mg
FOOD	
Type	**Variations**
Meats	Beef, chicken, pork, etc.
Fruits	Apples, strawberries, bananas, etc.
Vegetables	Brocoli, green beans, squash, etc.
Nuts & Seeds	Almonds, brazil nuts, cashews, etc.
EXERCISE	
Type	**Frequency**
Walking	6x a week
Weight lifting	2x a week

So first get yourself on a total brain-and-body health program. You'll start to feel really good physically. Then you can introduce and will be far more receptive to therapy. It's possible you might even discover that some of the things that have been bothering you aren't as bad as you thought they were.

If you find therapy intimidating, bear in mind that it doesn't have to be intensive. All you really need is a place you can go, sit, and honestly discuss what's going on in your life. You can talk about your worries, your fears, and your frustrations. If something set you off that week, you can talk about ways to avoid similar situations in the future. If you're facing big challenges, you can discuss how to tackle them. I personally continue to use therapy as a place to optimize myself.

Here's how I get the most out of each therapy session: Before my visit, I make a list of everything that might have upset me that week. Then, while I'm there, I discuss each item on the list with the therapist and get a professional opinion on how to solve my problems, even the small ones.

I'll give you some specific examples of ways therapy has helped me deal with ongoing problems. One week, I was going through an incredibly stressful time in my college career. Projects had piled up, finals were approaching, I had multiple assignments due, and I felt swamped. The stress started to build up, and when that happened, it began to affect my concentration and ability to get work done. It also manifested as physical symptoms, and I could feel the effects intensifying the longer I let the stress get to me.

When I went to my therapist that week, I was able to talk openly and at length about the things that were stressing me out. The therapist, in turn, helped me get to the root of the problem.

"Why are you getting so stressed out about this stuff? You know how to do this. Has it ever fallen apart in the past? Or if it has, haven't you always rebuilt it?"

Having a professional opinion navigating me through that week enabled me to deal with the stress, putting it in the proper perspective. I stepped back, took a look at all the tasks that had piled up, realized none of them were as difficult as they seemed, and was able to get through the rest of the week with no problems.

Therapy has also helped me immensely in my relationship with my girlfriend. My girlfriend and I have a proactive relationship: we don't wait for problems to occur before we deal with them. In other words, we're constantly laying the groundwork to deal with challenges that might come up. As a result, we've created a strong, healthy relationship, and we've never had any serious rocky patches. However, in every relationship, even healthy ones, issues will arise.

Occasionally, we experience a situation where we're not on the same page, something isn't clicking between us, or we just have a moment of tension. When that happens, therapy provides a place where I can go and talk through the issues, work out my feelings, and get some feedback about the healthiest ways to deal with them. My girlfriend and I always work through problems together, but therapy helps me on my end. Many small relationship problems become big ones because partners argue about them before they've really had a chance to work through their thoughts and feelings.

At the same time, in these weekly therapy sessions, I am constantly renewing my commitment to holistic health, so the sessions keep me on track. It's not that I need someone to keep me track. I don't. I am committed to this new lifestyle because of how it makes me feel, but it's good to have a place each week where I can center myself.

As long as you have a good therapist, one who is compassionate and thoughtful, there are no drawbacks.

CONCLUSION

—

If you're reading this book, chances are you're ready to make some radical changes in your life. You've finally gotten to the point where you're done feeling sick all the time. You're done feeling anxious and depressed. You want to get the most out of life, and you know that the way you're feeling isn't normal. This is not how life is supposed to be.

If you're a college student or young adult, now is the best time in your life to put some good habits into practice. You are making your own way and establishing the path you're going to take in life. Do it in the healthiest way possible. Eat, sleep, exercise, and talk your way to better brain health and a mind that's been healed.

Maybe you've suffered tremendous pain, and you're afraid you'll have to live with anxiety and depression for the rest of your life. That might even be what health-care professionals are telling you. Maybe all they're doing is trying to help you manage the symptoms, to hold them at bay without ever really getting rid of them. Maybe nobody has given you hope that you can be truly healed.

If that's the case, I'm here to tell you it's a lie. Don't buy into it. You are not meant to live on this earth feeling sick, sad, and miserable all the time. You are destined to flourish and thrive, to live a life of emotional and physical health.

If you've been made to think that you can't do anything about your situation, don't accept that diagnosis. Don't accept that your only hope for managing your misery is taking strong medication. You don't have to listen to what doctors are telling you.

Take a look around. Most of the people these doctors are treating aren't being healed. Many people with mental health problems don't improve through traditional medical treatment. You've probably known people like this. Maybe you're one of them. The medication isn't helping. Your anxiety and depression haven't gone away, and the meds are wreaking havoc on your body.

Aren't you ready to finally get to the root cause of these symptoms? Aren't you ready to finally fix these things? It's time to evaluate your life. Take a look at what you're putting into your body, and consider what it's doing to you.

If you're a young adult, you'll never have a better time to make the necessary changes. Now is the time to put yourself on the path to complete healing. Start giving your brain and body what they really need. Treat them the way they want to be treated, and reap the benefits.

It sounds like a simple process. That's because it is. The only reason you've never made these changes before is because you didn't realize the connection between your mind and your body. Nobody ever told you that your physical health is influencing your mental health, so it never occurred to you that the processed food you eat is contributing to your emotional struggles. Now, hopefully, you see this. Your brain runs everything in your body, and your body feeds your brain. That's the connection.

Once you begin to make the changes I've recommended, you are going to see results fairly quickly. Pay attention to and fully experience the healing. It's possible you've never imagined how much better life can be.

Yes, you can wake up every single day of your life feeling

amazing, ready to hop out of bed. You can get up and fill your body with fantastic food and nutrients and feel like you're in control again. Anxiety and depression will no longer run your life. You will feel like you've conquered them, truly and completely, for the first time. It's a new lease on life, filled with confidence and enthusiasm. I know, because I've lived it. I fell into the depths of mental health pain, and I broke my way out.

Make the changes now, because they will open up so many more opportunities in the future. At last, you will feel like doing all the things you never wanted to do when you were anxious and depressed. You will be able to make decisions about your future with a clear and excited mind.

Life can be everything you want it to be. Yours can be a life of health and pure joy. Yes, it's as simple as what you're eating, how much you're exercising, and how much you're sleeping. It really is that simple.

If you continue down the path you're on now, putting bad stuff into your body, you will continue to get bad stuff out. If you make radical changes and give yourself the good stuff you need, you're going to change everything. You're going find true healing—forever.

ABOUT THE AUTHOR

As a college student at Arizona State University, author and speaker EVAN MICHAEL YORK found himself sinking into a pit of anxiety and despair. He tried everything to improve his mental and emotional health, but traditional psychiatric treatment only made his condition far worse. After studying, researching, and ultimately experimenting on himself, he discovered a clear path to healing his brain and getting his life back. Having lived through a period of tremendous struggle and risen above it, he now shares what he's learned on the journey to a healthier life.